MORMON PANTRY

Saving Supper

Debbie G. Harman

Published by Covenant Communications, Inc.
American Fork, Utah

Printed in China
First Printing: March 2018

24 23 22 21 20 19 18 10 9 8 7 6 5 4 3 2 1

ISBN-13 978-1-52440-293-8

MORMON PANTRY
Saving Supper
Debbie G. Harman
SOY
PINTO BE
DAIRY
Shredded
MILD CHEDDAR
CREAM OF MUS
SOUR CREAM
CROCK-POT
RECIPES
LO
HI
OFF
WARM

Table Of Contents

In all of living have much of fun and laughter. Life is to be enjoyed, not just endured.

President Gordon B. Hinckley

Introduction

Although a great tip for saving on your grocery budget is to shop with coupons, this book is not about clipping coupons. This book is a basic guide on being more wise with basic meal planning and how to use the less expensive food items to stretch the more expensive foods.

Planning and preparing meals is one of the most basic and essential skills necessary and is often overlooked. Planning and preparing meals is more than knowing how to cook. Much of the family income can be wasted on food items if these skills are not known and used. How many times do we get busy with the demands of the day only to reach dinnertime and not know what to cook? We often resort to grabbing a pizza or throwing together a quick and convenient meal. Or we cook the convenient foods because that's all the kids will eat.

Not only will meal planning help with the budget, it will also help with picky eaters. When you prepare simple, basic meals on a consistent basis, children will respond to the consistency and they will enjoy the security of family mealtime—and ultimately become less picky in their eating habits.

Basic Budget Tips

Throughout this book there are many Budget-Savings Tips. Just like the few cents you save when using coupons, these tips are small and simple, but when you add them up they equal big savings.

1. Cut down or eliminate convenience food items from your grocery list.

   *Many people believe that meat is the most expensive food item. Although this might have been true a few decades ago, it certainly is not true now. Today, the most costly foods we purchase are "convenience foods." For example, 1 pound of beef costs, on average, about $4. A bag of potato chips (between 9 and 14 oz.) is more than $4. So you are paying about $6 a pound for "potatoes"! Try to eliminate prepackaged and processed foods from your menu plan.

   *Most bakery items fit into this convenience list. A dozen rolls, on average, costs more than $3, which means you are paying $3 a pound for flour. That doesn't seem like much for the convenience of grabbing a bag of rolls for your dinner. But if you consider how many times you purchase a bakery item to go with your meal, it is likely you are making this purchase three to four times a week, which equals $12 to $16 a week, or $48 to $64 a month. That is one-fourth of my entire food budget for six people! This book will show you just how easy it is to make all of your own bakery items.

   * For items other than meat and cheese, my rule of thumb is to not pay more than $1 per pound. Of course, there are times you will want to splurge to make a family favorite, but if you can plan most of your menu with this as your guide, you will begin to see huge savings in your grocery bill.

2. Stretch the meat in your menus and recipes.

* On average, we use too much meat in our daily diet. Not only is this not a healthy diet plan, it's also not a healthy budget plan. While meat is high in protein and other nutrients like vitamin B and iron, you can reduce the amount of meat you use and still maintain a very healthy diet. If you stretch the amount of meat used with other protein and vitamin-rich foods, you will not be at a health risk and you will notice a substantial change in your food budget.

* Combine other ingredients with the meat to stretch it. For generations, we have added oats, crackers, or bread crumbs to ground beef to make meatloaf, yet the thought of adding black beans to the same ground beef for hamburger patties seems unacceptable. Start adding beans to some of your meat dishes; you will not only save money but might discover some new family favorites like meat loaf.

* Use other food items such as potatoes, beans, pasta, rice, and other grains in your meal planning as a way of stretching your use of meat. For example, spaghetti noodles with a meaty marinara sauce is a family favorite and a great way to stretch ground beef into a very satisfying meal.

3. Use more fruits and vegetables!

* Plan your menu with seasonal vegetables in mind. We often plan our menu starting with the main dish. Try planning your menu with the vegetable first according to what is in season then pick a good main dish that goes well with that vegetable. You'll be surprised what a difference this will make

* Grow a garden and use more fruits and vegetables in your meal planning. Not only will this save you money but it will help children to be less picky eaters. Children need sugar, and if they do not get enough natural sugar they will crave sweets and treats. Refined sugar, however, ruins their appetites for dinner and turns them into very picky eaters. If you want them to eat better, use more fruits and vegetables in your meals.

Nutritional Essentials

PROTEIN: Protein builds, maintains, and replaces tissues in the body—especially muscles, organs, and the immune system. Protein makes hemoglobin (the part of red blood cells that carries oxygen to every part of the body). Protein is essential for the proper functioning of antibodies in resisting infection and for the regulation of enzymes and hormones. Lack of protein can cause growth failure, loss of muscle mass, decreased immunity, weakening of the heart and respiratory system, and death. Amino acids are the building blocks of protein. There are nine amino acids that the body cannot make; called essential amino acides, they need to be supplied in the diet.

Complete (Animal) Proteins: Proteins that have all nine of the essential amino acids.
Sources: Meat, poultry, fish, milk, cheese, yogurt, and eggs.

Incomplete (Plant) Proteins: Proteins that do not have all of the essential amino acids. Two incomplete proteins make up a complete protein. This means that when you eat two plant proteins, you will be getting all nine essential amino acids. However, this doesn't mean that even though whole grains have protein, if you ate two pieces of whole wheat bread you would be getting all of the essential amino acids. You must eat protein from at least two different sources within the day to make sure you are getting all nine of the essential amino acids.
Sources include: whole grains, beans, legumes, peas, nuts, peanut butter, spinach, kale, broccoli, sprouts, mushrooms, Brussels sprouts, and artichokes.

CARBOHYDRATES: Carbohydrates convert to glucose (sugar) for energy. If there is not enough glucose, the body will use protein for energy, thus robbing you of the vital amino acids that are essential for all functions of the body. But that isn't the only role of carbs. They also provide nutrients for the friendly bacteria in your intestinal tract that help digest food and they assist in the absorption of calcium.

Because many of the foods high in carbohydrates are also rich in fiber, they help lower cholesterol levels and regulate blood pressure. But if you eat more carbohydrates than your body can use in a day, that glucose will store as fat. This is why dieters try to avoid carbs. Don't avoid them; balance them with protein so that you have an adequate supply of both.

Essential Minerals

CALCIUM: Needed for healthy bones and teeth, helps blood to clot, helps nerves send messages for muscles to contract, and helps the brain comunicate with various parts of the body. Calcium deficiency can cause insomnia, weak and brittle nails, tooth decay, muscle cramps, and muscle aches, especially in the thighs, arms, and underarms. Most important, it can cause poor bone density.
Sources: Milk, yogurt, cheese, broccoli, mustard greens, beans, legumes, nuts, and black molasses.

IRON: Needed to help build muscles and maintain healthy blood by making the protein called hemoglobin.
Sources: Clams, organ meats (like liver), meat, soybeans, cereal, pumpkin seeds, beans, lentils, and spinach.

POTASSIUM: Helps regulate fluid levels, aids in muscular function and waste removal, and helps keep the nervous system functioning properly. Potassium helps reduce blood pressure and lowers risk for stroke. A deficiency in potassium can cause fatigue, insomnia, depression, muscle weakness, and many cardiovascular issues. Not enough potassium can cause muscle twitching, cramps, and muscle weakness.
Sources: Meats and fish, milk, avocados, potatoes, tomatoes, bananas, apricots, peaches, squash, dark leafy greens, figs, whole grains, beans, and legumes

ZINC: Needed for the immune system to work properly. It helps in cell division, cell growth, wound healing, and the breakdown of carbohydrates. It helps increase memory. Zinc is also needed for the senses of smell and taste and for fertility.
Sources: Seafood, spinach, whole wheat, cashews, beans, and dark chocolate.

PHOSPHORUS: Strengthens bones and teeth and boosts metabolism, which helps utilize carbohydrates, protein, and fat. Helps keep your muscles working, repairs tissues, and aids in all cell functions; it also regulates the heartbeat.
Sources: Meat, fish, poultry, eggs, and milk.

MAGNESIUM: Essential in preventing coronary artery spasms (a significant cause of heart attacks). Aids in protein and carbohydrate metabolism, relaxes muscles, aids in DNA functioning, and modulates the electrical potential across cell membranes (which allows nutrients to pass back and forth).
Sources: Dark green vegetables, nuts, seeds, legumes, soy products, avocados, apricots, dairy, meat, seafood. whole wheat, millet, and brown rice.

SULFUR: Essential for maintaining youthful skin and joints and a healthy digestive system. Sulfur makes up part of some of the amino acids involved in protein synthesis and several enzyme reactions. It helps produce collagen, which is a substance that forms connective tissues, cell structure, and artery walls. Sulfur is also a part of keratin, which is needed for strong hair, skin, and nails. Sulfur also fights fatigue, stress, and pain.
Sources: Eggs, meats, poultry, fish, milk, legumes, nuts, and garlic.

CHROMIUM: Aids in glucose function, making sure every cell in your body gets energy as it needs it.
Sources: Whole grains, fresh vegetables, and herbs.

Essential Vitamins

Vitamin A: Important for growth and development, maintenance of the immune system, good vision, bone metabolism, and for healthy bones, teeth, and skin. Also serves as an antioxidant.
Sources: Animal livers, butter, cheddar cheese, eggs, sweet potatoes, carrots, broccoli, kale, spinach, pumpkin, apricots, and cantaloupe.

Vitamin B_1 (Thiamin): Supports cellular energy production and normal nervous system function.
Sources: Lentils, whole grains, pork, milk, eggs, salmon, beef, spinach, and broccoli.

Vitamin B_2 (Riboflavin): Supports cellular energy production.
Sources: Milk, eggs, salmon, beef, spinach, and broccoli.

Vitamin B_3 (Niacin): Helps support cardiovascular (heart) health. Sources: Beef, poultry, fish, whole-wheat bread, peanuts, and lentils.

Vitamin B_5 (Pantothenic acid): Supports cellular energy production in the body. Prevents stomach problems and upper respiratory illness.
Sources: Organ meats (liver and kidney), egg yolks, whole grains, avocados, cashew nuts, peanuts, lentils, soybeans, brown rice, broccoli, and milk.

Vitamin B_6 (Pyridoxine): Needed to metabolize amino acids and glycogen (the body's storage form of glucose). Is also necessary for normal nervous system function and red blood cell formation.
Sources: Meat, poultry, eggs, bananas, fish, whole grains, and cooked spinach.

Vitamin B_7 (Biotin): Supports carbohydrate, protein, and fat metabolism as well as healthy hair, skin, and nails.
Sources: Strawberries, organ meats, cheese, and soybeans.

Vitamin B_9 (Folic acid): Supports fetal health and development (proper development of baby's nervous system). This important developmental process occurs during the initial weeks of pregnancy so folic acid intake is especially important for all women of child-bearing age. Sources: Dark leafy greens, asparagus, broccoli, citrus fruits, lentils, avocados, beans, lentils, seeds, and nuts.

Vitamin B_{12} (Cobalamin): Creates pathways that produce cellular energy. Also needed for DNA synthesis, proper red blood cell formation, and normal nervous system function.
Sources: Chicken, beef, fish, milk, and eggs.

Vitamin C: For growth and repair of tissues in all parts of the body. It helps the body make collagen (a protein used to make skin, cartilage, tendons, ligaments, and blood vessels). Needed for healing wounds and repairing and maintaining bones and teeth. It also helps the body absorb iron. Reduces the effects of sun exposure, such as sunburn or redness. It is an antioxidant. Antioxidants block some of the damage caused by free radicals (substances that damage DNA). The buildup of free radicals contributes to the the aging process and the development of health conditions such as cancer, heart disease, and arthritis.
Sources: Oranges, watermelon, papaya, grapefruit, cantaloupe, strawberries, kiwi, mango, broccoli, canned and fresh tomatoes, Brussels sprouts, cauliflower, cabbage, citrus juices, raw and cooked leafy greens, red and green peppers, potatoes, winter squash, raspberries, blueberries, cranberries, and pineapple.

Vitamin D: Needed for intestinal absorption of calcium, iron, magnesium, phosphate, and zinc.
Sources: Mackerel, salmon, tuna, sunlight on the skin, fortified milk.

Vitamin E: An antioxidant, it prevents oxidation of LDL cholesterol, needed for structure and maintenance of skeletal, cardiac, and smooth muscle; helps form red blood cells; and helps maintain stores of vitamins A and K, iron, and selenium.
Sources: Vegetable oils, avocados, spinach, sunflower seeds, wheat germ, nuts, and whole grains.

Vitamin F: Needed for nervous system functions and for skin suppleness and youthful appearance. Helps skin and hair stay shiny and healthy. Aids with skin allergies. depression, and fatigue.
Sources: Flaxseed oil, canola oil, soy oil, walnuts, sesame seeds, sunflower seeds, avocado, salmon, mackerel, sardines, and trout.

Vitamin K: Needed for the clotting of blood, bone health, and memory.
Sources: Kale, spinach, collards, Swiss chard, broccoli, Brussels sprouts, cabbage, asparagus (vitamin is higher in vegetables when cooked), whole-wheat flour, parsley, and green leaf lettuce.

Stocking the Pantry

BUYING AND STORING THE BAKING BASICS: Baking items usually go on sale during case lot sales, which are usually in the early spring and fall and during the end of November and December.

FLOUR—For the best bargain, purchase flour in 25-pound bags. Purchase whole-grain wheat in 50-pound bags.
ROLLED OATS—Purchase regular or quick in 25-pound bags.
SUGAR—For the best bargain, purchase sugar in 25-pound bags.
BROWN SUGAR—For the best bargain, purchase dark-brown sugar. If a recipe calls for light-brown sugar, mix half white sugar with dark-brown sugar.
POWDERED SUGAR—Not essential, but nice to have on hand. You can always make your own by grinding granulated sugar in a blender until it becomes a fine powder.
SALT—Purchase several cartons at a time, as salt will last indefinitely.
YEAST—Purchase in a block or jar and store in your refrigerator for longer shelf life.
BAKING POWDER—Baking powder has a shelf life of about 1 year. Stir 1/2 teaspoon baking powder into a cup of hot water. It will immediately start to fizz if it's still fresh.
BAKING SODA—Try the same test for freshness as instructed for baking powder, but add 1/4 teaspoon vinegar to the water before stirring in the baking soda.
VEGETABLE OIL—For best bargain, purchase gallon size and store in a cool, dark place for a longer shelf life.
POWDERED MILK—Purchase during case lot sales. Nice to have for bread recipes.
CANNED MILK—Not essential but nice to have on hand. You can use as a substitute for cream in soups and sauces.
NUTS and RAISINS—Not essential but good for some cereals, breads, and desserts.
VANILLA and MAPLE EXTRACT or IMITATION FLAVORING.
SPICES, such as CINNAMON, NUTMEG, GINGER, and CLOVES.
EGGS—Need to be refrigerated. You can purchase and store powdered eggs for baking but they are more expensive than raw eggs.
HONEY—Not essential, but better than sugar for whole-wheat breads. For best bargain, buy in buckets or large plastic bottles. If honey crystalizes, just redissolve by heating in microwave or in a pan of hot water on stovetop.
CORNMEAL—Purchase in 5- to 10-lb. bags as its shelf life isn't as long as flour.

CANNED FOODS: Best if you bottle your own, but otherwise, purchase when they go on sale (several times a year). Check local store ads and purchase by the case when you are able.

FRUITS AND VEGETABLES:

- CRUSHED TOMATOES, DICED TOMATOES, TOMATO SAUCE.
- WHOLE KERNEL CORN and GREEN BEANS (CUT and FRENCH-SLICED).
- DICED GREEN CHILIS.
- RIPE BLACK OLIVES.
- APPLESAUCE, MANDARIN ORANGES, PEACHES, PEARS, and PINEAPPLE.

CREAM OF CHICKEN and CREAM OF MUSHROOM SOUP.

FROZEN FOODS: Purchase in bulk when on sale (green peas, chicken, ground beef, sausage, and bacon).

DRY GOODS—These are also best to purchase during case lot sales.

- PASTA, such as SPAGHETTI, MACARONI, LASAGNA, and other NOODLES.
- RICE (BROWN and WHITE LONG-GRAIN)—Purchase in 20-pound. bags.
- BEANS, such as PINTO, SMALL RED, and BLACK—Purchase in 25-pound bags.

SEASONINGS, such as BAY LEAVES, BLACK PEPPER, GARLIC POWDER, ITALIAN SEASONING, OREGANO, PAPRIKA, PARSLEY , POULTRY SEASONING and THYME.

ENVELOPES of CHICKEN GRAVY, AU JUS, RANCH DRESSING, SLOPPY JOE SEASONING, AND TACO SEASONING.

PRODUCE—You will need to purchase produce weekly, but the items you should always keep on hand are ONIONS, POTATOES, CARROTS, CELERY, LETTUCE, and TOMATOES.

Recipes and Notes

Recipes and Notes

Meats and Potatoes

Nutritional Facts

White chicken meat is a complete protein and high in B-complex vitamins, which are needed for healthy skin, hair, eyes, and liver and also help the nervous system function properly. White chicken is a good source of choline, which is needed for brain function, and phosphorous, which is needed for bones and teeth, to keep muscles working, and to regulate heartbeat. Chicken is also a good source of selenium, which is an antioxidant and helps the thyroid. Chicken is an excellent source of potassium, which is essential for heart and muscle health. One serving of chicken breast provides almost 84 percent of the recommended daily allowance of this important mineral. Of the B vitamins, chicken is most noted for its excellent source of niacin (vitamin B3), which is essential for heart health and vital for converting carbohydrates into energy. One serving of chicken provides approximately 72 percent of the recommended daily allowance of niacin.

Dark chicken meat is also a complete protein source but is much higher in minerals than white chicken meat. Dark meat is a good source of vitamins A, K, and the B-complex vitamins. Dark chicken meat contains taurine, which significantly lowers the risk of coronary heart disease. Taurine may also help protect against diabetes and high blood pressure. For this reason, chicken soup from real chicken stock or a whole chicken is a far more nutitious choice.

Budget-Saving Tip

You can often find boneless chicken breasts for $1.49 per pound if you buy in large quantities. Place meat that will not be used the week of purchase in freezer zip-top bags or bottle the meat to use in your favorite recipes. Chicken legs and thighs with the bone and whole chickens regularly go on sale for $.59–.79 cents a pound. My personal limit for chicken is $1.89 a pound.

Nutritional Facts

Pork, like chicken, is a complete protein and an excellent source of thiamin, niacin, riboflavin, and vitamin B6. Next to milk, not many foods have as much riboflavin per serving as pork. Riboflavin helps release energy from foods. Pork, like dark chicken meat, is also a good source of phosphorus and zinc. Pork is the leading meat source of potassium; one boneless pork chop has about 750 milligrams.

Beef is also an excellent source of protein and of vitamin B12, niacin, vitamin B6, selenium, zinc, and phosphorus. In fact, beef is the #1 food source for protein, vitamin B12, niacin, vitamin B6, riboflavin, and zinc! It is also a good source of iron, potassium, copper, choline, pantothenic acid, and vitamin B2. For this reason, eating beef may be very beneficial after a surgery or having a baby, for recovering athletes, or during other conditions where muscle tissue is being built.

Budget-Saving Tip

To save money, you can combine pork with beef in many recipes. For example, when making a beef stew, use pork roast with your beef roast. A boneless pork roast is often $1.59 a pound, where a beef roast is at least $2.99 a pound. For spaghetti sauce, sloppy joes, meatloaf, etc., combine ground breakfast sausage with ground beef. (Sausage packaged by your store's butcher is far less expensive than the name brands.) I often buy sausage on sale for $1.59 a pound compared to the sale price of ground beef at $2.99 a pound. Not only will you save money, but the pork adds a nice flavor to beef recipes.

Basic Cooked Beef Roast

Bone-in or boneless beef rib eye, sirloin, rump, or chuck roast

Au Jus gravy mix and/or salt and pepper to taste

Slow-Cooker: Place beef in slow-cooker. Sprinkle with Au Jus gravy mix and/or salt and pepper. Cover and cook on high 4-6 hours or low 8-10 hours or until meat is tender. Discard bones, if any. Cool 30 minutes before slicing; return to slow-cooker to absorb juices. Use excess juice for gravy.

Oven: If desired, sear roast in a skillet in hot oil for 20-30 seconds on each side. Place roast in a baking pan. Sprinkle with Au Jus gravy mix and/or salt and pepper. Make a tent with foil over roast then cover pan with foil or lid. Bake at 350 for 30 minutes per pound for a medium roast.

If desired, use a meat thermometer to reach desired doneness:

Well-done: 155 degrees and above; brown color

Medium-well: 145-155 degrees; tan color, slightly pink

Medium: 135-145 degrees; rich pink color

Medium-rare: 130-135 degrees; bright red color

Rare: 120-130 degrees; bright purple-red (can't even think about it!)

Cool 20 minutes before slicing; return to baking dish to absorb juices. Use excess drippings when making gravy.

Roast, Potatoes, and Carrots

3- to 4-lb. beef roast (I prefer chuck)
Au Jus gravy mix
Salt and pepper to taste
8-12 medium potatoes, peeled, chopped
8-10 carrots, peeled, sliced
1 onion, diced (optional)

Prepare roast and cook in slow-cooker or oven according to instructions on opposite page. Sprinkle with Au Jus gravy mix and salt and pepper. For oven roast, place vegatables in roasting pan for last hour of cooking time. For slow-cooker roast, place vegetables in slow-cooker during last 2 hours on high or last 4 hours on low. Sprinkle vegetables with salt and pepper. Remove roast and let rest 20-30 minutes before slicing. Return to roasting pan or slow-cooker. Spoon juices over meat and vegetables before serving.

Mushroom Roast and Potatoes

Follow above recipe for Roast, Potatoes, and Carrots, using carrots if desired. Be sure to use the diced onion. Add potatoes, carrots (if desired), and onions when instructed during cooking time. After removing roast to slice, add 1 large can cream of mushroom soup and 1/2 soup can of milk. Stir well. Return sliced meat to roasting pan or slow-cooker and spoon mushroom gravy over meat. Heat through.

Basic Pork Roast

Bone-in or boneless pork shoulder or butt roast

Salt, pepper, and garlic powder to taste

Slow-Cooker: Place pork roast in slow-cooker, fat side down. Sprinkle with salt and pepper and garlic powder. Cover and cook on high 4-6 hours or low 8-10 hours or until meat is tender. Discard bones, if any. Cool 30 minutes before slicing; return to slow-cooker to absorb juices. Use excess juice for gravy.

Oven: Place roast in a baking pan, fat side up. Sprinkle with salt and pepper and garlic powder. Make a tent with foil over roast then cover pan with foil or lid. Bake at 300 for 40 minutes per pound and until inside temperature reaches 180 degreees. Discard bones, if any. Cool 30 minutes before slicing; return to pan to absorb juices. Use excess juice for gravy.

Pulled Pork Sandwiches

When pork roast is thoroughly cooked and tender, remove bones, if any, and excess fat from meat and slow-cooker. Leave roast in slow-cooker. Using two forks, pull pork apart to shred. Season to taste with salt and pepper, and chopped green onions if desired. Serve on hard rolls or hamburger buns spread with salad dressing or mayonnaise.

Easy Sweet Pulled Pork

For slightly sweet pork: Stir in 3/4 C. brown sugar for a 3- to 4-pouns roast. Heat through.

For tangy sweet pork: Add 1 C. salsa with the brown sugar. Heat through.

For sweet pork salad: Stir in 1 bottle black bean and corn salsa with brown sugar.

For barbecue pulled pork: Stir in 1 bottle barbecue sauce. Heat through. Serve on hard rolls or sliced French bread.

Mexican-Style Shredded Pork

- 3- to 4-lb. boneless pork roast
- 1 C. lemon-lime or root beer soda
- 1/4 C. Worchestershire sauce
- 1 10-oz. can red enchilada sauce
- 2 tsp. garlic powder
- 1/2 tsp. salt
- 1 tsp. black pepper
- 1/2 C. brown sugar

Place pork roast in a slow-cooker fat side down. Combine remaining ingredients except brown sugar; pour over roast. Cover and cook on high 4-5 hours or low 7-8 hours. Discard any excess fat from meat and slow-cooker. Return roast to slow-cooker. Using two forks, shred pork. Stir in brown sugar and cook withoout lid 30 minutes. Serve with your favorite Mexican dishes.

Slow-Cooker Norwegian Stew

1/2 lb. chopped bacon
2 onions, chopped
2-lb. beef roast
2-lb. pork roast
Salt and pepper to taste
10-12 potatoes, chopped

In a large skillet, cook bacon until almost crisp. Saute onions in bacon fat. Chop beef and pork roasts into bite-size chunks. Place meat chunks in slow-cooker. Sprinkle with salt and pepper. Spread onions and bacon over meat. Fill slow-cooker with chopped potatoes. Sprinkle with salt and pepper. Cover with water. Cook on high 3-4 hours or low 7-8 hours, until potatoes are tender and meat falls apart. Serve with ketchup and horseradish sauce.

Slow-Cooker Chicken Stew

4 chicken breasts
Salt and pepper to taste
6-8 carrots, sliced thick
8 potatoes, peeled and chopped
1 can cream of mushroom soup
1 C. sour cream

Place chicken breasts in slow-cooker. Sprinkle with salt and pepper. Layer on carrots and potatoes. Sprinkle with salt and pepper. Cover and cook on high 3 hours or low 5-6 hours. Check for dryness; add 1 C. water if needed. Remove chicken and cut into bite-size pieces. Return chicken to slow-cooker. Spread soup and sour cream over stew. Cover and cook 30 minutes.

Sanpete Marinated Turkey

4-6 lbs. turkey breast meat	1 C. soy sauce
2 C. 7-Up lemon-lime soda	1 T. garlic powder
1 C. vegetable oil	1 tsp. horseradish sauce (optional)

Cut turkey meat into 1- to 2-inch strips (like chicken strips). Combine remaining ingredients in a large bowl or container that has a lid. Stir in turkey meat until well coated. Cover and refrigerate 12–24 hours. Stir every 4–6 hours to marinate. Barbecue turkey meat over flame or broil in your oven a few inches from broiler until white on edges and insides are no longer pink. Boil or discard marinade, as it contains bacteria from the raw turkey meat. If desired, place grilled turkey in cooked marinade to keep moist.

Variation: You can use this marinade for chicken breast meat. Follow recipe as directed.

Sanpete barbecued turkey is served every year at the "Mormon Miracle" Pageant. This recipe is our family favorite for almost every get-together during the summer.

Basic Cooked Chicken

1 whole chicken, bone-in chicken breasts and/or thighs, or boneless chicken breasts
Poultry seasoning, chicken bouillon, salt, and pepper

Slow-Cooker Dry Method: My favorite way to cook chicken is in the slow-cooker. Place a whole chicken or a layer of chicken breasts or thighs in slow-cooker. Sprinkle with your choice of poultry seasoning, bouillon, salt, and pepper (you can also cook the chicken without any seasonings at all). Place another layer of chicken meat and repeat with seasonings. Cover and cook on high 3 hours or low 6-7 hours or until meat falls easily apart. If there are bones and skin, discard them. Cool slightly before tearing apart or chopping.

Slow-Cooker Poached Method: Follow directions above, but pour 1 quart water over chicken. Save liquid for broth and for storing chicken chunks to prevent drying out.

Stove Top: Follow recipe for poached method, but place chicken, seasonings, and water in a large soup pot (you can also cook a small amount of chicken in a saucepan). Bring to a boil over medium-high heat; reduce heat. Cover and simmer until chicken is tender and no longer pink (170 degrees F).

Whole Chicken: cook about 60 minutes.
Bone-in, skin-on chicken breasts: cook about 30 minutes.
Skinless, boneless chicken breast halves: cook 15-20 minutes.
Skinless, boneless chicken breast tenders: cook 10-15 minutes.

Oven, Whole Chicken: Place whole chicken in an oven bag or a brown paper bag. Place in a baking dish. Bake 30 minutes at 325 for each pound of chicken or until inside reaches 170 degrees as measured by a meat thermometer.

Oven, Cut Chicken: Place cut chicken pieces in a baking dish. Season as desired. Cover with foil. Bake at 350 for 45-60 minutes or until until chicken is tender and no longer pink.

Cornflake Chicken

4 boneless, skinless chicken breasts
1/2 stick butter, melted
2 C. cornflakes, crushed
1 tsp. garlic powder
Salt and pepper to taste
1/4 C. Parmesan cheese
1 C. yogurt or sour cream
1 can cream of chicken soup
1 soup can milk
2 T. parsley flakes

Cut chicken breasts in half to make 8 palm-size pieces. In a shallow bowl, blend melted butter, cornflakes, garlic powder, salt, pepper, and Parmesan cheese. Dip chicken pieces in yogurt then cornflake mixture and place in a greased baking dish. Bake at 350 for 1 hour.

To make chicken gravy, combine cream of chicken soup and milk in a saucepan. Cook over medium-low heat until hot and bubbly. Spoon over baked chicken when serving and sprinkle with parsley flakes.

Cornflake Chicken Casserole

Using ingredients above, cut chicken breasts in half to make 8 palm-size pieces. Place chicken in a greased baking dish. Combine yogurt or sour cream, cream of chicken soup, and milk. Spread over chicken. Bake at 350 degrees for 45 minutes. Combine cornflakes, garlic, salt, pepper, and cheese. Mix into melted butter and spread over chicken. Bake 15 minutes or until cornflakes start to brown.

Nutritional Facts

Potatoes are the number-one vegetable crop in the world! They are one of the cheapest universal crops to produce and are available year-round. One medium potato contains 164 calories, 0.2 grams of fat, 0 grams of cholesterol, 37 grams of carbohydrate, 4.7 grams of dietary fiber, and 4.3 grams of protein. One medium potato contains 2% of daily calcium, 51% vitamin C, 9% iron, 30% vitamin B6, 12% magnesium, and 25% potassium needs. Potatoes also provide phosphorus, niacin, folate, choline, and zinc.

The iron, calcium, phosphorous, magnesium, and zinc in potatoes help to build and maintain bone structure and strength. The high amounts of fiber, potassium, vitamin C, and vitamin B6, along with the fact that the potato has no cholesterol, make it good for the heart. And the fiber in potatoes prevents constipation and helps regularity. Potatoes function as a "bulking agent" in the digestive system to increase satiety and reduce appetite, making you feel fuller longer. They also contain a compound known as alpha-lipoic acid, which helps convert glucose into energy.

Potatoes contain phytonutrients (antioxidants) like carotenoids, flavonoids, and caffeic acid. Patatin, which stores the proteins in the potato, also fights against free radicals, Finally, the potato skin has a flavonoid called Quercetin, which is another antioxidant, making the potato a great food for helping prevent cancer. Quercetin is also a powerful anti-inflammatory agent.

New information is being found on the benefits of this root vegetable that was once thought to be toxic. Recently, scientists at the Institute for Food Research found blood-pressure-lowering compounds called kukoamines in potatoes. Kukoamines were previously found only in Lycium chinense, an exotic herbal plant used to make Chinese herbal medicine.

There is an unproven folk remedy for cold sores.

"Eat large amounts of potatoes every day!"

Believe it or not, recent research shows that potatoes do possess powerful antiviral properties. So if you suffer with cold sores, like my family does, you might want to try a potato diet!

Storing and Cooking Potatoes

Potatoes should be stored in a cool, dark, and dry area like a basement or pantry. Exposure to sunlight can cause the toxic compound solanine to form. Do not store potatoes in a cold area like the refrigerator. This causes the starch to convert to sugar, which changes the flavor. Potatoes should not be stored near onions because they both emit natural gases that cause the other to rot. Store-bought potatoes can be stored up to two months, but spoiled potatoes cause other potatoes to spoil. Remove rotted potatoes as soon as you see them.

When cooking potatoes on the stove top, always bring them to a boil, then reduce temperature and cook until tender. This will pevent them from becoming too starchy or sticky. Use the water potatoes have been cooked in to make your gravy. The starch helps thicken and flavor the gravy.

Since much of the vitamins, minerals, and fiber are in the skin, it is best to cook and eat potatoes with the skin left on. Although many recipes call for peeled potatoes, try them with the peels. I usually leave the peels on red potatoes, and I always eat the peels on baked potatoes. Scrub the potatoes under running water and remove any bruises or deep eyes with a paring knife or potato peeler. Cook or bake according to recipe.

Budget-Saving Tip

Many people buy frozen potatoes in the bag for the "convenience," but did you know that frozen potatoes are not cooked? They are frozen raw potatoes and take just as long to cook as potatoes you purchase from the produce section. Frozen potatoes cost as much as ten times the produce potatoes. I timed myself; it took two minutes to peel and chop six potatoes. You can save a lot of money in two minutes if you're willing to chop or grate your own potatoes. To make your own "convenience" potatoes, place several potatoes in a large pot. Cover with water and sprinkle salt over them. Bring to a boil. Reduce to medium and cook twenty minutes. Leave peels on. These potatoes may be stored in the refrigerator up to two weeks. They make cooking with potatoes a cinch!

Basic Baked Potatoes

Scrub 8-12 medium russet potatoes. For tender potato skins, wrap potatoes in foil. For crispy skins, do not wrap potatoes in foil. Place the potatoes on the middle oven rack. Bake at 425 for 45 minutes.

Baked Potato Bar

Follow recipe for Basic Baked Potatoes. Prepare desired toppings for potatoes, such as:

BUTTER and/or GARLIC BUTTER
SOUR CREAM and/or PLAIN YOGURT
RANCH DRESSING
SALT AND PEPPER
HERBS (chives, basil, cilantro, crushed red pepper)
CHOPPED GREEN ONIONS
SHREDDED CHEDDAR CHEESE
CHEESE SAUCE (page 67)
COOKED, CRUMBLED BACON
HAMBURGER GRAVY (page 16)
BEEF CHILI (page 45 or 1 15-oz. can chili con carne)
STEAMED BROCCOLI and/or SPINACH
SAUTEED VEGGIES (such as onions, mushroms, peppers)

Basic Mashed Potatoes

8-10 russet potatoes
1 1/2 tsp. salt
1 stick butter
1 c. milk
Salt and pepper to taste

Peel and chop potatoes in 1-inch chunks. Place in large pot and cover with water. Sprinkle with salt. Bring to a boil. Continue to cook until potatoes are just tender, about 15-20 minutes. Drain; return to pot. Add butter. Using a potato masher, mash slightly until butter is melted. Stir in milk, salt, and pepper. Whip with an electric mixer until smooth and fluffy.

Garlic Mashed Potatoes

6-8 large red potatoes
Salt to taste
1 stick butter
1 C. milk
1 1/2 tsp. garlic powder
Salt and pepper to taste

Chop but do not peel potatoes. Place in large pot and cover with water. Sprinkle with salt. Bring to a boil. Continue to cook until potatoes are just tender, about 30 minutes. Drain; return to pot. Using a potato masher, mash slightly. Add butter, milk, garlic powder, salt, and pepper. Stir with a woodlen spoon until butter is melted.

Steak and Mushroom Gravy

2 lbs. round steak
Cooking oil
All-purpose flour
1 can cream of mushroom soup

Cut steak into 2-inch pieces. Heat oil in heavy pan. Dip steak in flour, and brown in hot oil. Layer steak in slow-cooker. Add enough water to cover first layer. Cook on low 2-3 hours. If water boils away, add more so as to have 1 1/2 C. liquid for gravy. Stir in soup. Cook 30 minutes. Serve over mashed potatoes.

Hamburger Gravy

1 lb. hamburger
1 onion, finely diced
1/3 C. all-purpose flour
3 C. milk
1 4-oz. can mushrooms (optional)

Cook hamburger and onions in large skillet until meat is no longer pink. Do not drain fat. Add flour; cook and stir until flour forms a paste. Slowly stir in milk. Cook and stir until gravy thickens. If desired, fold in mushrooms. Heat through. Serve over mashed potatoes.

Chicken Fricassee Gravy

1/2 stick butter
1/3 C. all-purpose flour
3 C. milk
1 can chicken broth
1 T. dried parsley
2 C. chopped chicken

Melt butter in large saucepan. Add flour; cook and stir until flour forms a paste. Slowly stir in milk then chicken broth. Cook and stir until thickened. Add parsley and chicken and heat through. Serve over mashed potatoes.

Sausage Gravy

1 lb. breakfast sausage
1/3 C. all-purpose flour
3 C. milk
Salt and black pepper to taste

Cook sausage in large skillet until meat is no longer pink. Do not drain fat. Add flour; cook and stir until flour forms a paste. Slowly stir in milk. Cook and stir until thickened. Sprinkle with salt and a generous amount of pepper. Serve over mashed potatoes, biscuits, or toast.

Shepherd's Pie

1 lb. ground beef
1 onion, chopped
4 carrots, peeled and sliced
1 C. beef or chicken broth
2 C. frozen peas
3-4 C. leftover mashed potatoes

Brown ground beef, onion, and carrots in a large skillet over medium-high heat. Drain fat. Spread mixture in a 9x13 baking dish. Stir in broth and frozen peas. Spread mashed potatoes over meat mixture. Crosshatch top with fork. Bake at 350 for 30 minutes or until golden on top.

Variations: Replace frozen peas with 1 15-oz. can green beans, drained.
Replace fresh carrots and frozen peas with 12-oz. bag frozen vegetables.

THE HOME IS THE WORKSHOP WHERE HUMAN CHARACTERS ARE BUILT.

President Joseph Fielding Smith

Meatloaf Casserole

2 lb. ground beef
2 eggs, well beaten
1 8-oz. can tomato sauce
12 saltine crackers, crushed
1/2 tsp. garlic powder
1/2 tsp. Italian seasoning
Salt and pepper to taste
1 C. ketchup
3-4 C. mashed potatoes

Combine ground beef with eggs, tomato sauce, and cracker crumbs. Mix in seasonings and salt and pepper. Press into a 9x13 baking dish. Bake at 350 for 30-35 minutes or until meat is thouroughly cooked. Using a paper towel, dab to absorb extra grease. Spread ketchup over meatloaf. Broil on low until top is bubbly and darkened in color. Drop mashed potatoes by spoonful onto meatloaf (don't spread; you don't want potatoes to blend with ketchup). Place pan on lower rack in oven. Broil 5-7 minutes or until potato peaks turn golden brown.

Meatloaf and Fried Potatoes

Follow recipe for Meatloaf Casserole, but replace mashed potatoes with 6 potatoes, peeled and shredded. Fry shredded potatoes in 3 T. oil until browned, turning often. Sprinkle with salt and pepper. Continue to cook until potatoes are slightly crispy. Toss fried potatoes lightly over cooked meatloaf. Place pan on top rack: broil 1 minute.

Cheesy Fried Potatoes

6-8 potatoes, peeeled and shredded
3 T. vegetable oil
Salt and pepper to taste
1 C. shredded cheddar cheese
Barbecue sauce

Fry shredded potatoes in oil until browned, turning often. Sprinkle with salt and pepper. Continue to cook until potatoes are slightly crispy. Spread potatoes on a baking sheet. Sprinkle with cheese. Place pan on top rack: broil 1-2 minutes or until cheese is melted. Remove from oven and drizzle barbecue sauce over top. Serve immediately.

Twice-Baked Potatoes

6 medium russet potatoes, washed
6 T. butter
1/2 C. sour cream
1 C. grated cheddar cheese, divided
Salt and pepper to taste
6 slices bacon, cooked and crumbled
1 green onion, chopped, OR
1 T. thinly sliced chives

Place potatoes directly on oven rack. Bake at 425 for 45 minutes or until tender when pierced with a fork. Cut lengthwise in half. Leaving skins about 1/4 inch thick, scoop potatoes from skins into mixing bowl. Mix potatoes with butter, sour cream, 1/2 C. grated cheese, and salt and pepper. Place potato skins on a baking pan. Fill skins with potato mixture. Sprinkle with crumbled bacon, chives, or green onions and remaining grated cheese. Bake 10-15 minutes or until cheese is melted on top.

Pierogi Lasagna Rolls

8 lasagna noodles, cooked and drained
4 C. mashed potatoes
1 C. shredded cheddar cheese, divided
1 1/2 C. Alfredo sauce (page 67)
6 slices bacon, cooked and crumbled (optional)

Cut lasagna noodles into quarters. Spread 2 Tbsp. mashed potatoes on each noodle. Sprinkle with shredded cheese. Roll up and place in greased baking dish seam side down. Pour Alfredo sauce over lasagna rolls. Sprinkle with remaining cheese and bacon. Bake at 350 for 30 minutes.

Variations: Omit bacon. Replace Alfredo sauce with marinara sauce. Replace cheddar cheese with mozzarella cheese.

Stuffed Hot Dogs

3-4 C. leftover mashed potatoes
1 C. shredded cheddar cheese
12 hot dogs

Combine mashed potatoes and shredded cheese. Slice hot dogs lengthwise to open, but don't cut completely through. Place on baking sheet. Spoon mashed potatoes down centers of hot dogs. Bake at 400 for 10-15 minutes or until cheese is melted and hot dogs start to bubble.

Cheesy Potato Muffins

4 C. leftover mashed potatoes
1 egg, well beaten
1 C. shredded cheddar cheese, divided
3 green onions, chopped
Salt and pepper to taste

Stir together the mashed potatoes, egg, 3/4 cup shredded cheese, and green onions. Season with salt and pepper. Divide the potato mixture evenly into cups of a greased muffin tin. Bake at 375 for 30 to 35 minutes or until golden brown and crisp around the edges. Remove from oven and top muffins with remaining cheese. Bake 2-3 minutes or until cheese is melted on top. Let cool 5 minutes before removing from tin.

Bacon Cheese Muffins

Follow recipe for Cheesy Potato Muffins. Stir in 1 C. bacon bits into cheese and green onions. Continue as directed.

Family life should be a time of HAPPINESS AND JOY that children can look back on with fond memories and associations.

President Ezra Taft Benson

Yummy Potatoes

1 can cream of chicken soup
1 C. sour cream
2 C. shredded cheddar cheese
1 bunch green onions
Salt and pepper to taste
6-8 potatoes, boiled, peeeled, and shredded
2 C. cornflakes crushed
1/2 stick butter, melted

In a 9x13 baking pan, combine soup, sour cream, cheese, and green onions. Sprinkle with salt and pepper. Fold in potatoes. In a medium bowl, mix cornflakes and melted butter. Spread over potatoes. Bake, uncovered, at 350 for 30 minutes.

Ham and Potato Gratins

1 medium onion, chopped
1/4 C. butter
Salt and pepper to taste
4-6 medium potatoes, peeled and sliced
2 C. leftover glazed ham
2 C. grated cheese
2 T. chopped fresh parsley
2 C. half-and-half

Saute onion in butter until tender. Sprinkle with salt and pepper. Combine with potatoes, ham, cheese, and parsley. Spread mixture in a 9x13 baking dish. Pour half-and-half over potatoes. Cover with foil and bake 30 minutes. Uncover and bake 35 additional minutes.

Potato Spinach Kielbasa

- 4 red potatoes, cubed
- 3 cloves garlic, minced
- 1/2 lb. Kielbasa or Italian sausage
- 1/2 tsp. dried oregano
- 1/2 tsp. dried thyme (optional)
- Salt and pepper to taste
- 5 strips bacon, cooked and crumbled
- 4 C. fresh baby spinach

Place potatoes in pot. Cover with water and sprinkle with salt. Bring to a boil. Reduce heat to medium and continue to cook until potatoes are just tender. Drain. Meanwhile, saute garlic in bacon grease until you can smell the garlic. Stir in sausage and drained potatoes. Stir-fry until potatoes are browned on edges. Sprinkle with seasonings, salt, and pepper. Add crumbled bacon and spinach. Cover and simmer until spinach wilts.

Vegetable Medley Potatoes

Follow recipe for Potato Spinach Kielbasa but omit the bacon and sausage. Replace spinach with 4 C. chopped broccoli and carrots. Steam broccoli and carrots with potatoes until crisp-tender. Drain. Stir-fry vegetables and garlic in 1/4 C. butter until potatoes are browned on edges. Sprinkle with seasonings, salt, and pepper.

TIP: Boil a pot of unpeeled potatoes, sprinkled with salt. Store them up to two weeks in the refrigerator for quick use in potato casseroles and other potato dishes.

Tin Foil Dinners

2 lb. ground beef
1 onion, diced
2 eggs, well beaten
1 8-oz. can tomato sauce
12 saltine crackers, crushed
1/2 tsp. garlic powder
Salt and pepper to taste
4-6 potatoes, peeled and diced
4 carrots, peeled and sliced
2 C. frozen peas

Combine first 7 ingredients. Tear off 8 squares of foil. Form meat mixture into 8 patties. Layer meat, potatoes, carrots, and peas on each on each piece of foil. Season with salt and pepper. Fold up sides of foil and seal at top. Place foil pouches on a broiling pan to collect drippings. Bake at 350 for 30 minutes or until meat is cooked through.

Chicken Foil Dinners

1 lb. chicken breast tenders
4-6 potatoes, peeled and grated
4 carrots, peeled and grated
1/2 C. ranch dressing
Italian seasoning
1/3 C. shredded Parmesan cheese
Salt and pepper to taste

Spray 8 squares of foil with non-stick spray. Divide chicken, potatoes, and carrots and place on foil squares. Drizzle with ranch dressing and sprinkle with Italian seasoning, cheese, and salt and pepper. Follow cooking directions for Tin Foil Dinners.

German Potato Salad

2 lbs. red potatoes, unpeeled, chopped
6 slices bacon, chopped
1 onion, diced
1/2 C. chicken stock
1/4 C. apple cider vinegar
1/2 C. green onions, chopped

Place potatoes in a large pot. Cover with water. Sprinkle with salt. Bring to a boil. Reduce temperature to medium and cook 15-20 minutes or until potatoes are tender. Drain potatoes. Meanwhile, cook bacon in a skillet until done. Remove bacon; saute onion in bacon grease until tender. Stir chicken stock, vinegar, and cooked potatoes into sauteed onions. Cook and stir until potatoes have absorbed the liquid. Stir in bacon and green onions.

Curry Potato Salad

8 potatoes, peeled, diced
6 eggs, hard-boiled, diced
2 green onions, chopped
3-4 ribs celery, diced
3 whole pickles, diced
2 radishes, grated (optional)
3/4 C. mayonnaise
1/4 C. ranch dressing
1 tsp. curry powder
1/2 tsp. paprika
Salt and pepper to taste

Place potatoes in a large pot. Cover with water. Sprinkle with salt. Bring to a boil. Reduce temperature to medium and cook 15-20 minutes or until potatoes are tender. Drain potatoes. In a large mixing bowl, combine potatoes with all other ingredients; salt and pepper to taste.

8 russet potatoes
1 C. salad dressing
3-4 Tbsp. prepared mustard
1 C. finely diced dill pickles
1/4 C. pickle juice
4 eggs, hard-boiled, divided
1 onion, finely diced
Salt, pepper, and paprika to taste

Place potatoes in a large soup pot. Cover with water and sprinkle with salt. Bring to a boil. Reduce heat to medium. Cover and cook 20 minutes or until potatoes are just tender. Drain. Combine salad dressing, mustard, pickles, and pickle juice. Using a hand-held grater, grate cooked and cooled potatoes and 3 hard-boiled eggs. Stir potatoes, eggs, onions, and desired amount of salt and pepper into salad. Slice remaining hard-boiled egg and place egg slices on top of salad. Sprinkle with paprika.

...AND YE WILL TEACH YOUR CHILDREN TO LOVE ONE ANOTHER, AND TO SERVE ONE ANOTHER.

MOSIAH 4:15

Recipes and Notes

Beans and Legumes

Nutritional Facts

Beans are a super-healthy, super-versatile, and super-affordable food. One cup of cooked beans provides 15 grams of protein, making them one of the best sources of plant protein. Beans are also rich in fiber. In addition to lowering cholesterol, the high fiber content of beans prevents blood sugar levels from rising too rapidly after a meal, making them a good choice for people with diabetes, insulin resistance, or hypoglycemia. They are high in antioxidants and prebiotics. Prebiotics move through the digestive tract until they reach the colon, where they are fermented by beneficial bacteria, stimulating their growth. Research studies have shown that prebiotics may improve colon health and reduce the risk of colon cancer. Eating beans regularly may also decrease the risk of diabetes, heart disease, colorectal cancer,and help with weight management. Beans are also an excellent source of vitamins B1, B6, and folic acid. Folic acid reduces the risk of birth defects of a baby's brain and spine by 50 to 70 percent. Folic acid may also lower the risk of preeclampsia and early labor. Lack of folic acid causes anemia. One cup of cooked beans has 0 grams of fat, 40 percent of the daily requirement of copper, and 38 percent of the requirement of manganese. Manganese is required for proper enzyme functioning, nutrient absorption, wound healing, and bone development. Beans contain 29 percent of the daily recommended amount of zinc.

Budget-Saving Tip

Add beans to your menu to stretch your food dollars. Beans can be added to soups and salads as well as many meat dishes and casseroles. Dry beans cost between seventy-five cents and a dollar per pound. When you consider that they triple in bulk and weight when cooked, this wonder food can be as cheap as twenty-five cents per pound. That will really make a difference in the budget!

Cooking Dry Beans

You don't need to soak beans! I have been cooking beans for more than thirty years without soaking them and they always turn out wonderful! And you don't have to sort them to remove the broken beans. For years my husband and I debated this topic. As a boy, he had to sort the beans before his mother soaked them. He grew up in Ajo, Arizona, which is next to the border of Mexico. They cooked a lot of beans! I don't remember how my mother cooked beans because she rarely did. Occasionally she made Boston baked beans in the oven, but I can't recall if she soaked them first. She probably did, but because I didn't know it was a step in the process and because we received a slow-cooker as a wedding gift, I just put some beans in it and cooked them. Thirty years later, that is howI still cook them.

You can cook beans on the stove top or in the oven, but the two ways that we cook our beans is in a slow-cooker or, when we're in a hurry, in a pressure-cooker.

Slow-Cooker Method: Place 2 C. or 1 lb. dry beans in a slow-cooker. Pour 2 quarts water over beans. Season as desired with salt and pepper, spices, vegetables,and/or meat (like salt pork, bacon, or hamhocks). If you are making chili or another recipe that calls for uncured meat such as hamburger or chicken, put the meat in after the beans are thoroughly cooked or the meat will lose its flavor. Cover and cook on high 4-8 hours (depending on beans) or until beans are tender, but not bursting.

Pressure-Cooker Method: Place 2 C. or 1 lb. dry beans in a pressure-cooker. Pour 2 quarts water over beans. Season as desired with salt and pepper, spices, vegetables,and/or meat. Be sure to not fill the pressure cooker above the halfway mark (beans expand when cooking). Place lid on and lock to secure. Pressure cook for 20-30 minutes. Check for doneness (release pressure quickly by placing cooker under cold running water).

Note: When cooking dry beans, do not add tomato sauce, vinegar, or anything acidic until beans are completely cooked and tender. The acidity prevents the beans from absorbing water and softening.

Slow-Cooker Baked Beans

12 oz. bacon, chopped
2 C. dry small white beans
2 quarts water
1 tsp. each salt and pepper
1 onion, peeled and diced
3/4 C. molasses
2 T. dry mustard
1 C. ketchup (optional)

In a skillet, cook bacon; pour cooked bacon and grease into slow-cooker. Add beans and water. Sprinkle with salt and pepper. Cover and cook on high 4 hours. Add diced onion, molasses, and dry mustard. Cook 2 hours more or until beans are tender but not falling apart. If desired, stir in ketchup. Heat through.

Quick Baked Beans

6 slices bacon, cooked and crumbled
1/2 onion, diced
1/2 green bell pepper, diced
3 15-oz. cans pork and beans
1/2 C. ketchup
1/2 C. brown sugar
2 T. mustard
Salt and pepper to taste

Saute onions and bell peppers in bacon grease until tender. Drain liquid from 2 cans of pork and beans; discard liquid. Combine all ingredients in a 9x13 baking dish. Bake uncovered at 350 for 30 minutes.

Hawaiian Baked Beans

- 6 slices bacon, cooked and crumbled
- 1 onion, diced
- 1 green bell pepper, diced
- 3 15-oz. cans pork and beans
- 1/2 C. ketchup
- 1/2 C. brown sugar
- 1 T. Worcestershire sauce
- 1 15-oz. can pineapple chunks, drained

Saute onions and bell peppers in bacon grease until tender. Drain liquid from 2 cans of pork and beans; discard liquid. Combine all ingredients in a 9x13 baking dish. Bake uncovered at 300 for 1 hour.

Baked Bean Casserole

- 1 lb. hamburger, cooked and drained
- 4 slices bacon, cooked and crumbled
- 1 onion, diced
- 1 green bell pepper, diced
- 2 15-oz. cans pork and beans: drain 1 can
- 1 15-oz. can kidney beans, drained
- 1/2 C. ketchup
- 1/2 C. brown sugar
- 1 T. Worcestershire sauce
- 2 T. mustard

Combine all ingredients in a 9x13 baking dish. Bake at 350 for 30 minutes.

Mashed Bean Meatloaf

2 eggs
1 C. mashed pinto beans
1/4 C. onion, chopped
1/4 C. green bell pepper, chopped
1 tsp. garlic powder
Salt and pepper to taste
1 lb. ground beef
1 C. ketchup

Combine eggs, beans, onion, peppers, garlic powder, and salt and pepper. Fold in ground beef. Press meat mixture into a loaf pan. Bake at 350 for 30 minutes. Spread ketchup over the top. Bake 10 minutes more.

Variation: Substitute 1 C. cooked lentils for the pinto beans.

Black Bean Burgers

1 15-oz. can black beans, drained
3/4 C. seasoned bread crumbs
1/2 tsp. garlic powder
1 large egg
1/4 tsp. cumin
Salt and pepper to taste

Place black beans in a bowl; partially mash with a fork. Stir in remaining ingredients. Stir until well combined. Form mixture into patties (like hamburgers). Pour small amount of oil into a large skillet. Cook patties over medium-high heat 2–3 minutes on each side or until burger is heated through. Serve on buns with condiments as you would hamburgers.

Variation: Add 1 lb. ground beef to bean mixture.

Pinto Bean Sloppy Joes

2 lb. ground beef
1/2 onion, diced
2 ribs celery, diced
1 15-oz. can pinto beans, drained
1/2 env. sloppy joe seasoning
1 15-oz. can crushed tomatoes
3 T. sugar
8-12 hamburger buns

Cook ground beef, onions, and celery until meat is done. Drain excess fat. Stir in remaining ingredients. Simmer over low heat 30 minutes.

Marvelous Meatballs

2 eggs
1 C. mashed pinto beans
1/4 C. onion, chopped
1 lb. ground beef
1 tsp. garlic powder
Salt and pepper to taste
1 can cream of mushroom soup
1 soup can milk

Combine all ingredients except soup and milk. Shape into balls. Brown in small amount of fat. Transfer meatballs to a baking dish. Combine soup and milk. Pour over meatballs. Bake at 350 for 30 minutes.
Serve over hot cooked noodles or rice.

A MAN SHOULD NEVER NEGLECT HIS FAMILY FOR BUSINESS

Walt Disney

Fried Pinto Bean Tacos

2 C. pinto beans
1/2 C. grated Monterey Jack cheese
1/2 C. cornmeal
2 T. green onions, finely chopped
1 T. cilantro, finely chopped
1/8 tsp. ground cumin
1 large egg
1 T. vegetable oil

In a bowl, use a fork to partially mash pinto beans. Add remaining ingredients except oil. Stir until well combined. In a large skillet, heat oil over medium-high heat. Add mixture to pan; cook 7–8 minutes, stirring often and allowing pieces to clump together like hamburger. Serve in warm tortillas with greens and pico de gallo.

Traditional Fried Bean Tacos

Follow recipe for Fried Pinto Bean Tacos but omit the green onions and cilantro. Replace cumin with 1/2 pkg. taco seasonong. Serve in tortillas with sour cream, guacamole, lettuce, and salsa or pico de gallo.

Easy Guacamole

Cut avocados in half. Remove pits. Scoop avocado meat from skins. Sprinkle with pinch of salt. Mash with a fork then stir until smooth.

Hamhock and Beans

1 leftover hamhock
1 tsp. garlic powder
2 quarts water
2 C. great northern beans
Salt and pepper to taste

Place all ingredients in a slow-cooker. Cover and cook on high 4–6 hours or low 8–10 hours, until beans are tender but not falling apart. Remove hamhock. Pull any ham left on bone and return meat to slow-cooker; discard bone.

Variation: Substitute small white beans or pinto beans for the great northern beans.

Slow-Cooker Refried Beans

2 strips bacon, chopped
2 C. dry pinto beans
1 tsp. salt
1/2 tsp. pepper
1 tsp. garlic powder
2 quarts water

Place all ingredients in a slow-cooker. Cover and cook on high 4–6 hours or low 8–10 hours, until beans are tender but not falling apart. Mash beans to desired consistency. Serve with your favorite Mexican or Southwest dishes.

Variation: This recipe can also be made without the bacon.

Taco Quiche

1 lb. ground beef
1/4 C. onion, chopped
1/4 C. green pepper, chopped
1 env. taco seasoning
1 C. shredded cheddar cheese
1/2 C. flour
1 tsp. baking powder
1/2 tsp. salt
2 eggs, beaten
1 C. milk

Brown ground beef with onion and green pepper over medium heat until meat is no longer pink; drain. Add taco seasoning; stir until well combined. Spread in a greased casserole dish. Sprinkle with cheese. In a bowl, sift the flour, baking powder, and salt. Stir in eggs and milk; mix well. Pour over the cheese. Bake at 400 for 20-25 minutes or until a knife inserted near the center comes out clean. Serve with salsa, lettuce, tomatoes, and other taco toppings.

Variation: Stir 1 C. pinto, black, kidney, or refried beans into meat mixture with the taco seasoning until well combined. Continue as directed.

The most important work you and I will ever do will be within the walls of our own Homes.

President Harold B. Lee

Taco Casserole

1 lb. ground beef
1/2 onion and 1/2 green pepper, diced
2 C. pinto, black, or red beans, drained
1 C. shredded cheddar cheese
1 C, sour cream
4 C. corn chips, slightly broken

Brown ground beef with onion and green pepper over medium heat until meat is no longer pink; drain. Season with salt and pepper. Combine with beans, shredded cheese, and sour cream in a 9x13 baking dish. Fold in chips. Bake at 350 for 30 minutes. Serve with salsa.

Bean and Veggie Nachos

4 C. corn chips
2 C. refried beans
1 C. shredded cheddar cheese
1 C. sour cream
Lettuce, finely shredded
Onions, tomatoes, and peppers, diced
Ripe black olives, sliced
Salsa

Spread corn chips evenly on a baking sheet. Drop dollops of beans onto chips. Sprinkle with cheese. Broil 3-4 minutes or until cheese is melted and bubbly, Divide onto individual plates. Top with sour cream, lettuce, onions, tomatoes peppers, olives, and salsa.

Tamale Pie

1 lb. ground beef
1 onion, finely diced
1 8.5-oz. pkg. cornbread mix
1/2 tsp. cumin
1 tsp. chili powder
1 15-oz. can pinto beans
1 15-oz. can corn or cream-style corn
1 4-oz. can diced green chilis
1 15-oz. can enchilada sauce
2 C. shredded cheddar cheese

Brown ground beef with onion. Drain fat. Season with salt and pepper, Set aside. Make cornbread mix according to package directions or make cornbread from recipe on page 138. Pour cornbread batter into a greased 9x13 baking dish. Combine meat with spices, beans, corn, and chilis. Spread meat mixture over cornbread batter. Pour enchilada sauce over top and sprinkle with shredded cheese. Bake at 400 for 20 minutes.

Beef and Bean Enchiladas

Cook 1 lb. ground beef with garlic powder, salt, and pepper. Drain fat. Combine meat with 1 15-oz. can refried beans. Spread mixture down centers of 10-12 corn or flour tortillas. Place in a 9x13 baking dish. Pour 3 C. red enchilada sauce over top. Sprinkle with 2 C. shredded cheddar cheese. Bake at 350 for 30 minutes. Serve with your favorite toppings.

Black Bean Enchiladas

3 C. red enchilada sauce, divided
1 onion, diced
1 bell pepper, diced
1 tsp. vegetable oil
1 15-oz. can corn, drained
1 15-oz. can black beans, drained
8-10 corn or flour tortillas
2 C. shredded cheddar cheese, divided

Spread 1 C. enchilada sauce in a 9x13 baking dish. Sauté onions and peppers in hot oil until tender. Add corn and beans. Spread 1/2 C. mixture down center of each tortilla. Sprinkle with cheese; roll up and place in baking dish. Top with remaining sauce and shredded cheese. Bake at 350 for 30-40 minutes or until cheese is melted and bubbly.

Variation: Substitute green enchilada sauce for the red enchilada sauce.

Chili Chicken Enchiladas

1 15-oz. can small white beans
1 10-oz. can cream of chicken soup
1 4-oz. can diced green chilis
1 C. sour cream
2 C. shredded cheddar cheese
1 C. chopped, cooked chicken
10 corn tortillas, torn into 2-inch pieces

Combine ingredients in order given in a 9x13 baking dish. Bake at 350 for 30 minutes.

Chicken Chili

2 lbs. chicken thighs
2 14.5-oz. cans chicken broth
1 medium onion, finely diced
2 15-oz. cans small white beans
1 4-oz. can diced green chilis
Salt and pepper to taste

Place chicken thighs in slow-cooker. Pour chicken broth over chicken. Cover and cook on high 2 hours. Remove skin and bones from chicken; discard. Cut chicken into bite-size pieces. Return to slow-cooker. Add remaining ingredients. Cook on high 1 hour. Serve with corn tortilla chips and choice of toppings.

Taco Soup

1 lb. ground beef
1 medium onion, chopped
1 28-oz. can crushed tomatoes
1 10-oz. can Rotel tomatoes
1 15-oz. can corn, drained
1 15-oz. can black beans, rinsed
1 15-oz. can pinto beans, drained
1 env. ranch dressing mix
1 env. taco seasoning
1 1/2 C. water

Brown ground beef with onion. Drain fat. Stir in tomatoes,corn, beans, seasonings, and water. Bring to a boil. Reduce heat. Simmer 30 minutes. Top individual servings with cheese and sour cream. Serve with tortilla chips.

Italian Chili

1 lb. ground beef
1 onion, diced
1/2 green bell pepper, diced
2 ribs celery, diced
1 tsp. garlic powder
1 tsp. Italian seasoning
1 tsp. chili powder
1 quart V-8 juice
2 14.5-oz. cans Italian tomatoes
2 15-oz. cans kidney beans, drained
2 15-oz. cans white beans, drained
1 C. macaroni noodles

Brown ground beef with onion, green pepper, and celery. Drain excess fat. Season with salt and pepper. Stir in remaining ingredients except macaroni noodles. Simmer over medium heat. Meanwhile, cook macaroni according to package directions. Stir into soup. Heat through. Serve with hard rolls or French bread.

FAMILY LIFE IS THE BEST METHOD FOR ACHIEVING HAPPINESS IN THIS WORLD.

President Spencer W. Kimball

Tuscan White Bean Soup

1 onion, finely diced
2 medium carrots, finely diced
2 ribs celery, finely diced
2 T. olive oil
4 cloves garlic, minced
1/2 tsp. dried red pepper flakes
1 quart chicken broth
2 15-oz. cans white beans with liquid
2 bay leaves (optional)
3-4 C. kale or Swiss chard, chopped
1 C. half-and-half
Parmesan cheese for serving

Sauté onion, carrots, and celery in hot oil until onions turn clear. Stir in garlic; cook 30 seconds. Add remaining ingredients except half-and-half and cheese. Sprinkle with salt and pepper. Simmer 30 minutes. Remove bay leaves. Stir in cream. Serve with Parmesan cheese.

Ham and Bean Soup

3 carrots, peeled and shredded
3 potatoes, peeled and finely diced
1 onion, finely diced
2 C. ham, cubed
2 15-oz. cans white beans
1 tsp. each salt and pepper
1/2 C. brown sugar
Dash cinnamon or nutmeg
4 C. water

Combine all ingredients in a soup pot. Cook 20 minutes over medium heat.

Slow-Cooker Chili

2 C. small red beans
1 env. chili seasoning mix
2 qt. water
1 lb. hamburger, cooked and drained
2 C. salsa or 1 15-oz. can crushed tomatoes or tomato sauce

Place first 3 ingredients in slow-cooker. Cook on high 4-6 hours or until beans are tender but not falling apart. Stir in cooked meat and salsa. Cover and cook 30 minutes.

Busy Day Chili

1 lb. ground beef
1 onion, diced
1 small green pepper, chopped
2 T. chili powder
1/2 tsp. ground cumin
1 quart V-8 juice
2 15-oz. cans small red beans, drained
1 15-oz. can kidney beans, drained

In a soup pot, cook ground beef with onion and green pepper until meat is done. Drain fat. Season with salt and pepper. Stir in remaining ingredients. Simmer for 10 minutes.

Seashell Bean Soup

3 slices bacon, chopped
1 onion, finely diced
6 cloves garlic, minced
1 28-oz. can whole tomatoes with juice
2 C. chicken broth
1 tsp. dried oregano
1 15-oz. can small red beans
1 15-oz. can kidney beans
2 bay leaves
1 C. seashell pasta
Salt and pepper to taste
2 T. fresh parsley leaves, chopped

Cook bacon and onion in bacon grease until onions turn clear. Stir in garlic; cook 30 seconds. Add remaining ingredients except parsley. Sprinkle with salt and pepper. Simmer 30 minutes. Remove bay leaves. Stir in fresh parsley leaves.

Let love, and peace, and the Spirit of the Lord,
kindness, charity, sacrifice for others,
abound in your families.

President Joseph F. Smith

Lentil and Rice Pilaf

1 C. green or brown lentils
2 1/2 C. water
2 C. onions, finely chopped
2 T. olive oil
1 tsp. garlic, minced
3/4 C. long-grain white rice
1 tsp. salt
3/4 tsp. ground cumin
1/2 tsp. pepper
1 14.5-oz. can chicken broth

Dump lentils into a soup pot. Add water. Bring to a boil. Cover and simmer until tender, 20–25 minutes. Drain. In a separate pot, sauté onions in hot oil until onions start to brown. Add garlic, rice, salt, cumin, and pepper; cook and stir until rice looks opaque, about 3 minutes. Stir in lentils and chicken broth. Bring to a boil; reduce heat. Simmer, covered, for 20 minutes.

Chicken Broccoli Pilaf

Follow recipe for Lentil and Rice Pilaf, but cut 1 chicken breast into bite-size chunks. Sauté chicken chunks with onion until edges turn white. Continue as directed, but add 2 C. chopped broccoli and 1 C. water to rice mixture. Cook as directed.

Recipes and Notes

Soups and Stews

Basic Chicken Stock

2 lbs. chicken thighs and legs
1 large onion, quartered
2 ribs celery, cut into 2-inch pieces
2 carrots, unpeeled, cut into 2-inch pieces
3 cloves garlic, smashed
2 bay leaves
10 sprigs thyme
Salt and pepper to taste

Place all ingredients and 3 quarts water in a slow-cooker. Cover and simmer on low 8 hours. Remove meat from bones; store for later use. Discard bones, skin, and vegetables. Strain broth using a fine-mesh strainer. Allow to cool before pouring into containers. Store in refrigerator up to 5 days or in freezer up to 6 months.

Basic Beef Stock

4 lbs. beef bones (ask butcher)
2 carrots, unpeeled, cut into 2-inch pieces
1 medium onion, quartered
2 celery stalks, cut into 2-inch pieces
2 bay leaves
Salt and pepper to taste

Place all ingredients and 3 quarts water in slow-cooker. Cover and simmer on low 8 hours. Discard bones and vegetables. Strain broth using a fine mesh strainer. Allow to cool before pouring into containers. Store in refrigerator up to 5 days or in freezer for up to 6 months.

French Onion Soup

2 onions, thinly sliced
2 T. butter
1 quart beef broth
1 1-oz. pkg. Au Jus gravy mix
Garlic croutons
Mozzarella cheese, grated

In a soup pot, sauté onions in butter until brown. Stir in beef broth and Au Jus gravy mix. Simmer 15 minutes. Top individual servings with croutons and cheese.

Steak and Mushroom Soup

Salt and pepper to taste
1 lb. beef sirloin or ribeye, thinly sliced
2 T. oil, divided
1 onion, thinly sliced
2 C. mushrooms, sliced
2 minced garlic cloves
4 T. all-purpose flour
2 15-oz. cans beef broth
1 C. grated mozzarella cheese (optional)

Sprinkle salt and pepper on steak. Sear meat in 1 T. hot oil. Set aside. Saute onions in remaining oil until onions begin to brown. Add mushrooms and garlic. Continue to sauté until you can smell the garlic. Stir in flour to make a paste. Slowly stir in beef broth. Cook and stir until thickened. Add seared steak and simmer on low for 10 minutes. If desired, top individual servings with mozzarella cheese.

Basic Chicken Noodle Soup

1 whole chicken
2 quarts water
4-6 carrots, sliced
4 ribs celery, sliced
1 onion, diced
2 C. uncooked noodles
1/2 C. chopped parsley
Salt and pepper

Place chicken and water in large soup pot. Bring to a boil. Reduce heat; cover and simmer until chicken is cooked through, 20-30 minutes. Using tongs, remove chicken. Cool slightly. Discard skin and bones. Cut chicken into bite-size pieces; set aside. To broth, add carrots, celery, and onion. Simmer 15 minutes. Add noodles, parsley, and chicken. Simmer until noodles are tender. Season to taste with salt and pepper.

Homemade Egg Noodles

1 1/3 C. flour
1 tsp. salt
2 eggs
2 T. vegetable oil
2 T. water

Mix flour and salt. In a separate bowl, barely mix egg, oil, and water. Stir into flour. Knead until smooth. Let rest 10 minutes. Roll very thin. Let dry 20 minutes. Cut into thin strips with pizza cutter. Add to boiling soup or boiling water. Cook until tender; 7 minutes.

Yummy Vegetable Beef Stew

2 lbs. boneless chuck roast, cubed
2 onions, chopped
4 ribs celery, chopped
6-8 carrots, chopped
Salt and pepper to taste
1 6-oz. can tomato paste
1 1/2 quarts beef broth, divided
1 bag frozen peas or green beans (optional)
2 bay leaves

Put first 6 ingredients plus 1/2 quart broth in slow-cooker. Cover and cook on high 3-4 hours or low 7-8 hours. Add frozen peas or green beans, bay leaves, and remaining broth. Cook an additional 20 minutes. Remove bay leaves before serving.

Variation: Replace frozen peas with 2 C. chopped cabbage. Cook until cabbage is tender.

Beef and Noodle Soup

Follow above recipe for Vegetable Beef Stew, but increase to 2 quarts beef broth. Cook 4 cups medium egg noodles from recipe on opposite page or according to package directions. Stir uncooked noodles into boiling soup; cook until tender.

Minestrone Soup

- 1 onion. chopped
- 2-3 celery ribs, sliced
- 3 small zucchini, sliced
- 2 T. butter
- 1 quart beef stock or broth
- 1 15-oz. can white beans
- 1 15-oz. can cut green beans
- 1 48-oz. can tomato juice
- 1 tsp. Italian seasoning
- 1/2 tsp. garlic powder

In a soup pot, sauté onion, celery, and zucchini in butter until onion becomes clear. Add remaining ingredients. Simmer 30 minutes.

Soup is a lot like a family. Each ingredient enhances the others, each batch has its own characteristics, and it needs time to simmer to reach full flavor.

Margaret Kennedy

Creamy Clam Chowder

1 onion, finely diced
4 ribs celery, finely diced
1/2 stick butter (1/4 C.)
4 potatoes, peeled and cubed
2 cans minced clams
2 C. water
Salt and pepper to taste
2 C. half-and-half

In a soup pot, sauté onions and celery in butter until onions are clear. Add potatoes and cook 2-3 minutes or until potatoes start to cook on edges. Drain clam juice into potatoes without adding clams. Add water and sprinkle with salt and pepper to taste. Simmer 15-20 minutes until potatoes are tender. Mash potatoes slightly. Stir in clams and half-and-half. Heat through.

Creamy Corn Chowder

Follow recipe for Clam Chowder, but replace butter with 6 slices bacon, cooked and crumbled. Remove bacon, and sauté onions and celery in bacon grease. Replace minced clams with 2 C. fresh, frozen, or canned corn. Add corn with potatoes and continue as directed. Garnish with crumbled bacon.

Variation: Add 2 small cans diced green chilis with the corn.

Favorite Hamburger Soup

2 lbs. lean ground beef
1 onion, diced
3 ribs celery, sliced
3 C. carrots, peeled and sliced
4 potatoes, peeled and diced
8 C. water
1 tsp. celery seed
Salt and pepper to taste
1/4 C. Worcestershire sauce
1 C. frozen corn
1 C. frozen peas

Cook ground beef with onion and celery. Drain excess fat. Add carrots, potatoes, water, and seasonings. Bring to a boil. Simmer 30 minutes or until veggies are tender. Add Worcestershire sauce, corn, and peas. Heat through.

Cheeseburger Soup

Follow recipe for Favorite Hamburger Soup, but do not drain fat from cooked hamburger. Stir in 1/4 C. flour until it forms a paste. Add 3 C. beef broth and 1 1/2 C. milk until well blended. Add 4 red potatoes, chopped. Bring soup to a boil. Reduce heat and simmer 12-15 minutes or until potatoes are tender. Stir in 1 C. shredded cheese and 1/2 C. sour cream. Heat through and serve hot.

Chicken and Spinach Soup

2 chicken breasts
1 onion, finely diced
2 C. chicken broth
5 C. baby spinach, chopped
2 pkgs. chicken gravy mix
2 C. half-and-half

Place chicken and diced onions in a soup pot. Pour broth over top. Bring to a boil. Reduce heat. Cover and simmer 20 minutes. Remove chicken and cut into bite-size chunks. Return to pot. Add spinach and simmer until tender. Meanwhile, combine gravy mix and half-and-half. Slowly stir into soup. Cook and stir until thickened.

Budget-Saving Tips

Making soup is a great way to save food dollars, but here are a few tips that will save you even more:

If you don't want to purchase cream or half-and-half, you can thicken your cream soup with potatoes, flour, or cornstarch. Or stir in 1/4 C. bean flour (beans ground into powder from processing in the blender). Allow to boil 5 minutes in your pot of soup. This will make the soup thick and creamy. Extend cream soups by adding a cup or more of milk.

You can reduce meat and cheese in soups by adding extra sautéed or fresh onions and/or garlic.

Use an envelope of gravy mix when a recipe calls for a can of cream soup. It's less than half the price, and your family won't even notice the difference.

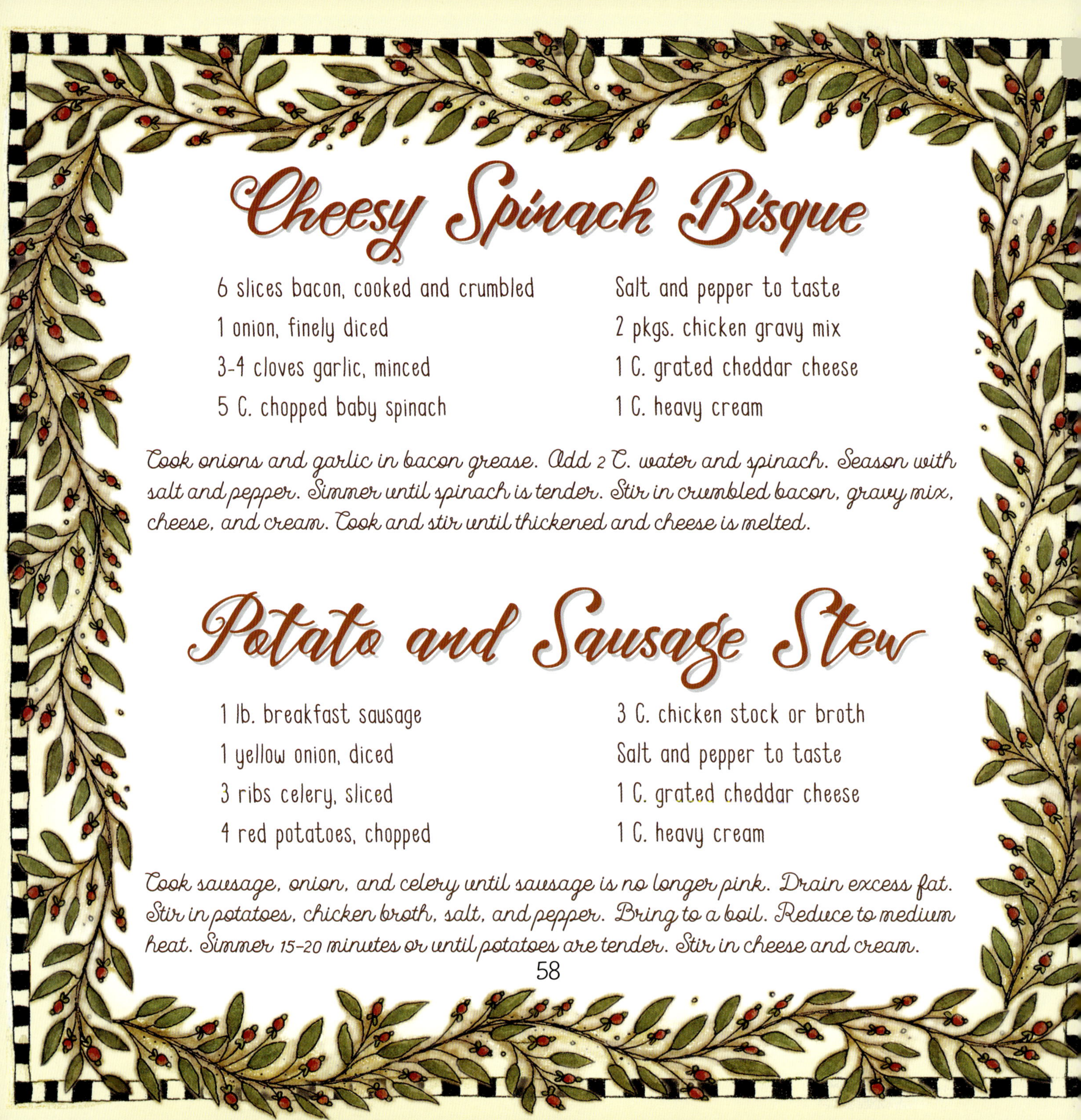

Cheesy Spinach Bisque

- 6 slices bacon, cooked and crumbled
- 1 onion, finely diced
- 3-4 cloves garlic, minced
- 5 C. chopped baby spinach
- Salt and pepper to taste
- 2 pkgs. chicken gravy mix
- 1 C. grated cheddar cheese
- 1 C. heavy cream

Cook onions and garlic in bacon grease. Add 2 C. water and spinach. Season with salt and pepper. Simmer until spinach is tender. Stir in crumbled bacon, gravy mix, cheese, and cream. Cook and stir until thickened and cheese is melted.

Potato and Sausage Stew

- 1 lb. breakfast sausage
- 1 yellow onion, diced
- 3 ribs celery, sliced
- 4 red potatoes, chopped
- 3 C. chicken stock or broth
- Salt and pepper to taste
- 1 C. grated cheddar cheese
- 1 C. heavy cream

Cook sausage, onion, and celery until sausage is no longer pink. Drain excess fat. Stir in potatoes, chicken broth, salt, and pepper. Bring to a boil. Reduce to medium heat. Simmer 15–20 minutes or until potatoes are tender. Stir in cheese and cream.

Sausage and Kale Soup

6 slices bacon
1 lb. pork sausage
1 onion, diced
4 cloves garlic, minced
4 potatoes, peeled and cubed
1 quart chicken broth
2 C. water
Salt and pepper to taste
3-4 C. chopped kale
2 C. half-and-half

In a soup pot, cook bacon until crisp. Remove bacon and crumble. Set aside. Cook sausage, onion, and garlic in bacon grease until sausage is no longer pink. Stir in potatoes, chicken broth, water, and salt and pepper. Bring to a boil. Reduce to medium heat. Add kale and simmer 15-20 minutes or until potatoes are tender. Stir in half-and-half and crumbled bacon.

Broccoli Potato Soup

4 potatoes, peeled and cubed
2 stalks broccoli
1/2 tsp. chicken boullion
1/2 tsp. each salt and pepper
1 can cream of chicken soup
1 C. sour cream

Place potatoes and broccoli in a soup pot. Sprinkle with chicken bouillon and salt and pepper. Cover and simmer until potatoes are tender. Mash slightly. Stir in soup and sour cream; warm through.

- 2 C. fresh or frozen broccoli, chopped
- 1 quart chicken broth
- 2 env. chicken gravy mix
- 1/4 C. powdered cheese
- 4 C. milk
- 1/2 C. shredded cheddar cheese

Steam broccoli in broth until tender. In a separate pan, combine gravy mix, powdered cheese, and milk. Cook and stir until thickened. Stir in broccoli and shredded cheese. Cook until hot and bubbly.

Baked Potato Soup

- 1 stick butter (1/2 C.)
- 1/2 C. all-purpose flour
- 4 C. milk
- 6 baked potatoes, peeled and cubed
- 1 lb. bacon, cooked and crumbled
- 3 C. shredded cheddar cheese
- 2 C. sour cream
- 1 bunch green onions, chopped
- 1 T. salt
- 1 T. ground black pepper

Melt butter in soup pot. Add flour and stir until it forms a paste. Stirring continuously, slowly pour in milk and stir until smooth. Reduce to medium heat. Add remaining ingredients. Stir occasionally, making sure to scrape bottom of pot, until cheese is melted and soup is warmed through. Yummy with bread bowls.

Creamy Zucchini Soup

1/2 C. finely diced onion
3-4 medium zucchini, sliced
3 T. butter
Salt and pepper to taste
2 env. chicken gravy mix
4 C. milk
2 C. shredded cheddar cheese

Sauté onions and zucchini in butter until squash is tender but still firm. Season with salt and pepper. Remove from pan. Combine gravy mix, milk, and cheese. Cook and stir until thickened and cheese is melted. Fold in zucchini. Heat through.

Quick Tomato Soup

1/4 C. butter
1/4 C. all-purpose flour
2 8-oz. cans tomato sauce
4 C. water
2 T. sugar
Salt and pepper to taste

Melt butter. Stir in flour until it forms a paste. Slowly stir in tomato sauce, then water and sugar. Cook and stir over medium heat until soup begins to boil and is slightly thickened. Season to taste with salt and pepper.

Tastes great served with grilled cheese sandwiches!

Vegetable Alfredo Soup

2 boneless, skinless chicken breasts
1 quart chicken broth
4 garlic cloves, minced
1 lb. baby carrots
1 onion, diced
1 red bell pepper, diced
1 C. chopped broccoli
2 C. heavy cream
1 T. fresh basil, snipped
Fresh Parmesan cheese, grated

Place first six ingredients in slow-cooker. Cover and cook on high 3-4 hours or low 6-7 hours or until meat is thoroughly done. Remove chicken and cut into bite-size chunks. Meanwhile, add broccoli to slow-cooker. Cook additional 30-40 minutes or until broccoli is tender. If needed, season with chicken bouillon. Add chicken and cream; heat through. Stir in basil. Sprinkle with Parmesan cheese when serving.

Pasta Alfredo Soup

Follow above recipe, but cook 2 C. bow-tie or rotelle pasta according to package directions; drain. Stir into soup. Serve with Parmesan cheese.

Tortellini Stew

9 oz. fresh or frozen tortellini
2 large carrots, finely chopped
2 medium zucchini, sliced
1 T. olive oil
2 T. minced garlic
1 tsp. oregano
Salt and pepper to taste
1 quart beef broth
2 C. baby spinach or chopped kale
Parmesan cheese

Cook tortellini according to package directions. Drain. In a soup pot, sauté carrots and zucchini in olive oil 5 minutes. Add garlic and sauté 1 minute. Add oregano, salt and pepper, broth, and spinach. Simmer 15 minutes. Stir in cooked tortellini. Warm through. Sprinkle individual servings with Parmesan cheese.

How long has it been since you
took your children, whatever their size,
in your arms and told them that you
love them and are glad
that they can be yours . . . forever?

President Spencer W. Kimball

Recipes and Notes

Pasta and Rice
SWEET
SOY SAUCE

Basic Marinara Sauce

1 T. olive oil
2–3 cloves garlic, minced
2 15-oz. cans crushed tomatoes
Fresh thyme, basil, and oregano
2 T. sugar
1/4 tsp. salt

Sauté garlic in warmed oil until fragrant, about 30 seconds. Add remaining ingredients. Simmer 10–15 minutes or until sauce begins to darken.

Variation: *You can substitute 1 tsp. garlic powder and 1 tsp. dried Italian seasoning for the garlic cloves and fresh hetbs. Cook as directed.*

Spaghetti Sauce

1 lb. ground beef
1/2 lb. ground sausage (optional)
4-5 cloves garlic, minced
Salt and pepper to taste
3 15-oz. cans crushed tomatoes
1/4 C. sugar
1 T. Italian seasoning

In a large pot, cook meats with garlic, salt, and pepper to taste. Drain excess fat. Stir in remaining ingredients. Simmer 10–15 minutes or until sauce thickens and turns deep red in color. Use this sauce for spaghetti, lasagna, or other favorite recipes.

Basic Alfredo Sauce

1 stick butter
2 C. heavy cream
1 C. grated Parmesan cheese
1/4 tsp. each salt and pepper

Melt butter in a heavy skillet over medium-low heat. Stir in cream and simmer 5 minutes. Stir in Parmesan cheese, salt, and pepper.

Garlic Alfredo Sauce: *Add 2 cloves minced garlic with butter and cream.*

Basic White Sauce

1/2 stick butter
1/4 C. all-purpose flour
2 C. milk
Salt and pepper to taste

Melt butter in a skillet. Stir in flour until it forms a paste. Slowly stir in milk. Cook and stir until thickened. Season with salt and pepper.

Garlic Alfredo Sauce: *Add 1/2 tsp. garlic powder with the butter.*
Basic Cheese Sauce: *Stir 1 C. grated cheddar cheese into white sauce.*

Favorite Spaghetti

Cook 8 oz. spaghetti noodles according to package directions. Follow Spaghetti Sauce recipe from previous page. Serve over cooked noodles; sprinkle with Parmesan cheese.

Baked Lasagna

- 4 C. spaghetti sauce, divided
- 9 lasagna noodles, divided
- 1 24-oz. container cottage cheese, divided
- Parsley flakes, divided
- Parmesan cheese, divided
- 1 C. grated mozzarella cheese, divided

Cook lasagna noodles according to package directions. Drain. In a 9x13 baking dish make 2 layers each of 1 C. spaghetti sauce, 3 lasagna noodles, and 1 1/2 C. cottage cheese. Sprinkle both layers with parsley flakes and cheeses. Top second layer of cottage cheese with 3 noodles, spaghetti sauce, and remaining mozzarella cheese. Bake at 350 for 30 minutes. Allow to sit 10-15 minutes before serving.

Slow-Cooker Lasagna

Follow recipe from Baked Lasagna but do not cook the lasagna noodles. Break uncooked noodles to fit slow-cooker. Make layers of sauce, noodles, and cheese as directed. Cover and cook on high 2-3 hours or low 6-7 hours. Allow to cool 30 minutes before serving.

Lasagna Soup

1 lb. lean ground beef
1 onion, diced
4-5 garlic cloves, minced
1/2 tsp. red pepper flakes
4 15-oz. cans crushed tomatoes
2 qt. chicken broth
2 T. Italian seasoning
1 T. garlic powder
1/4 C. granulated sugar
Salt and pepper to taste
10 uncooked lasagna noodles, broken
1 C. grated Parmesan cheese
1 C. grated mozzarella cheese

Cook meat and onion in large soup pot over medium-high heat until meat is browned. Add garlic and red pepper flakes and sauté for 30 seconds. Drain excess fat. Stir in crushed tomatoes, chicken broth, seasonings, sugar, and salt and pepper. Bring to a boil. Add lasagna noodles. Boil 5 minutes. Reduce temperature and simmer, stirring occasionally, 20 minutes or until lasagna noodles are tender, Sprinkle tops of idividual servings of soup with Parmesan and mozzarella cheese.

Variations: Any pasta can be substituted for the lasagna noodles in this recipe.
This recipe can be made with or without the meat.
Add 1 C. sautéed mushrooms with the tomato sauce and seasonings.

Basic Macaroni and Cheese

2 C. macaroni noodles
1/4 C. butter
1/4 C. all-purpose flour
1 C. milk
1 C. grated cheddar cheese

Cook macaroni according to package directions. Drain. Melt butter in pan. Add flour and stir until it forms a paste. Whisking continuously, slowly pour in milk and stir until smooth. Reduce to medium heat. Add cheese and stir until melted. Fold in macaroni noodles.

Variation: Baked Macaroni and Cheese
Follow above recipe. Spread prepared macaroni and cheese in a 9x13 baking dish. Sauté 2 C. bread crumbs in 1/4 C. butter until well coated. Sprinkle bread crumbs over macaroni and cheese. Bake at 350 for 20 minutes.

Grandpa's Mac 'n Cheese

Prepared macaroni and cheese
1 pkg. hot dogs, sliced into 1/2-inch circles

Follow above recipe for Macaroni and Cheese. Fry hot dog circles in a skillet until edges are browned. Stir into prepared Macaroni and Cheese.

*** Grandpa's Mac 'n Cheese tastes the best served with pork and beans!

- 2 C. macaroni noodles
- 1 15-oz. can chili con carne
- 1 15-oz. can corn, drained
- 1 C. sour cream
- 1 C. grated cheddar cheese

Cook macaroni according to package directions. Drain. Combine all ingredients in a 9x13 baking dish. Bake at 350 for 30 minutes.

Tuna Pasta Casserole

- 3 C. macaroni noodles
- 2 cans tuna fish, drained
- 1 can cream of celery soup
- 1/2 soup can milk
- 2 C. frozen peas
- Salt and pepper to taste
- 3 C. crushed potato chips

Cook macaroni according to package directions. Drain. In a 9x13 baking dish, combine tuna, soup, and milk. Fold in cooked macaroni and peas. Sprinkle with salt and pepper. Spread crushed chips over the top. Bake at 350 for 30 minutes.

Beef Stroganoff Casserole

4 C. egg noodles
1 lb. hamburger, cooked and drained
Salt and pepper to taste
1 T. Worcestershire sauce
2 15-oz. cans green beans, drained
1 can cream of mushroom soup
1 C. sour cream

Combine all ingredients in a 9x13 baking disk. Bake at 350 for 30 minutes.

Cowboy Casserole

3 C. macaroni noodles
1 lb. hamburger, cooked and drained
1 onion, finely diced
1 T. Worcestershire sauce
1 15-oz. can black beans, drained
1 15-oz. can diced tomatoes
1 15-oz. can corn, drained
1 C. grated cheddar cheese

Cook macaroni according to package directions. Drain. Combine all ingredients in a 9x13 baking dish, Sprinkle with salt and pepper. Bake at 350 for 30 minutes.

Beef Stroganoff

1 lb. sirloin steak, cubed
1/2 onion, diced
1/2 tsp. garlic powder
Salt and pepper to taste
1/4 C. all-purpose flour
2 C. beef broth
1 C. sour cream
1 3-oz. can mushrooms

In a large skillet, cook steak and onions until meat is done. Season with garlic powder, salt, and pepper. Stir in flour until meat is well coated. Gradually add beef broth. Cook and stir until thickened. Stir in sour cream and mushrooms. Serve over cooked egg noodles or rice.

Easy Beef Stroganoff

1 lb. hamburger, cooked and drained
Salt and pepper to taste
1/2 tsp. garlic powder
1 can cream of mushroom soup
1 C. sour cream
1 T. Worcestershire sauce

Combine all ingredients. Cook until hot and bubbly. Serve over cooked egg noodles.

Chicken Milano

8 oz. fettuccini noodles
2-3 chicken breast halves
2 T. vegetable oil
2 cloves garlic, minced
1/2 C. sun-dried tomatoes, chopped
1 C. chicken broth
1 C. heavy cream
2 T. chopped fresh basil

Cook fettuccine according to package directions. Drain and set aside. Sprinkle chicken on both sides with salt and pepper to taste. In a large skillet over medium heat, sauté chicken in oil 4-5 minutes per side or until the meat feels springy and is no longer pink. Remove chicken and set aside. Add garlic to skillet; cook 30 seconds. Stir in tomatoes and chicken broth. Bring to a boil. Reduce heat and simmer, uncovered, 10 minutes or until tomatoes are tender. Add cream. Cook and stir over medium heat until sauce thickens. Stir in basil. Cut each chicken breast into 2 to 3 diagonal slices. Serve pasta with chicken and cream sauce on top.

ONLY WHEN THERE IS UNSELFISHNESS WILL LOVE, WITH ITS CONCOMITANT QUALITIES, FLOURISH AND BLOSSOM.

President Gordon B. Hinckley

Creamy Shrimp Alfredo

1 lb. medium shrimp, peeled and deveined
1 T. vegetable oil
2 C. Alfredo sauce (page 67)
1 C. cherry tomatoes, halved
2 C. baby spinach leaves
8 oz. fettuccine noodles, cooked, drained
2 T. grated Parmesan cheese

Cook shrimp in hot oil over medium-high heat, stirring occasionally, until shrimp turns pink; about 5 minutes. Remove and set aside. Prepare Alfredo sauce, in same skillet, according to recipe. Stir in tomatoes and spinach. Cook 5 minutes or until spinach wilts. Stir in shrimp and fettuccine until well coated. Sprinkle individual servings with Parmesan cheese.

Bacon Cabbage Pasta

6 slices bacon
3 carrots, peeled and grated
4 C. thinly sliced green cabbage
1 onion, diced
3 C. egg noodles, cooked and drained
Salt and pepper to taste
1/2 C. Parmesan cheese

Cook bacon in large skillet until crisp. Remove from pan and crumble. Remove excess fat. Stir-fry vegetables in 2 T. bacon grease. Return bacon to skillet. Stir in cooked egg noodles. Sprinkle with salt and pepper and Parmesan cheese. Stir to coat.

Easy Fettuccine Alfredo

1/2 lb. fettuccine noodles
1/2 stick butter
1 tsp. garlic powder
1 C. heavy cream
1/2 C. grated romano cheese
1/2 C. grated Parmesan cheese

Cook pasta according to package directions. Drain. Melt butter and garlic in pan. Return noodles to pan and stir to coat with butter, Sprinkle with salt and pepper to taste. Add remaining ingredients. Cook and stir until cream is absorbed and cheese begins to melt.

Grilled Chicken Alfredo

1/2 lb. fettuccine noodles
2 chicken breasts, cut into strips
Italian seasoning
Garlic powder
Salt and pepper to taste
Alfredo sauce (page 67)

Cook pasta according to package directions. Drain. Sprinkle chicken strips with Italian seasoning, garlic powder, salt, and pepper. Grill chicken or stir-fry in hot olive oil until chicken is done. Place a few chicken strips on individual servings of cooked noodles. Drizzle with warm Alfredo sauce.

Artichoke Chicken and Pasta

- 8 oz. fettuccine noodles
- 1 T. olive oil
- 2 chicken breast halves, thinly sliced
- 1 14-oz. can artichoke hearts, chopped
- 2 C. Alfredo sauce (page 67)
- 1/2 C. crumbled bacon (optional)
- 1 large tomato, seeded and chopped
- 1 T. fresh basil leaves, chopped
- 1/2 C. shredded asiago or mozzarella cheese

Cook fettuccine according to package directions. Drain. Heat oil in large skillet over medium-high heat. Cook chicken in hot oil until thoroughly cooked. Remove and set aside. Add artichoke hearts to same skillet and cook over medium-high heat, stirring occasionally, about 2 minutes. Add Alfredo sauce, chicken, bacon, and tomatoes. Heat through. Stir in noodles until well coated. Remove from heat; stir in basil and sprinkle with cheese. Cover and let stand until cheese melts.

Spinach and Artichoke Chicken

Follow recipe for Artichoke Chicken & Pasta, but stir in 2 C. fresh baby spinach with the artichoke hearts. Continue as directed.

Variation: You can prepare both of these dishes without the chicken.

Chicken Zucchini Alfredo

- 2 chicken breasts, cut into strips
- Lemon pepper
- Garlic Alfredo Sauce (page 67)
- 1/2 onion, finely diced
- 2 medium zucchini, thinly sliced
- 4 Roma tomatoes, cut into wedges
- Fresh basil, chopped
- 1 lb. fettuccine noodles, cooked and drained

Season chicken with lemon pepper and grill or stir-fry. Prepare Alfredo sauce according to recipe. Sauté onion and zucchini in 1 T. hot oil until tender. Stir in tomatoes and basil. Fold chicken and zucchini mixture into Alfredo sauce. Serve over cooked noodles.

Chicken Mushroom Alfredo

- 1 1/2 lbs. chicken, chopped
- 1 C. mushrooms, sliced
- 1/4 tsp. garlic powder
- Salt and pepper to taste
- 1 stick butter, melted
- 2 8-oz pkg. cream cheese, softened
- 2 C. milk
- Fettuccini noodles, cooked
- 1 C. Parmesan cheese

Place chicken and mushrooms in greased slow-cooker. Sprinkle with garlic powder, salt, and pepper. Combine butter, cream cheese, and milk until smooth. Pour over chicken. Cover and cook on low 4-5 hours. Serve over fettuccine noodles. Sprinkle with Parmesan cheese.

Buffalo Chicken Pasta

1 lb. chicken, cubed
1 tsp. each salt and pepper
1 tsp. garlic powder
1 tsp. paprika
2 T. hot sauce
1 C. mayonnaise
1/2 C. ranch dressing
3/4 C. milk
1 lb. penne pasta, cooked and drained
1 C. shredded cheddar cheese

Season chicken with salt, pepper, and spices. Cook chicken in hot oil until no longer pink. Stir in hot sauce. Set aside. In a small bowl, stir mayonnaise, ranch dressing, and milk. Add sauce to chicken; heat through. Stir pasta into sauce. Top with cheese.

Bacon Cabbage Pasta

6 slices bacon
1 onion, diced
3 carrots, peeled and grated
4 C. thinly sliced green cabbage
3 C. egg noodles, cooked and drained
1/2 C. Parmesan cheese

Cook bacon in large skillet until crisp. Remove from pan and crumble. Remove excess fat. Stir-fry vegetables in 2 T. remaining bacon grease. Return bacon to skillet. Stir in cooked egg noodles. Sprinkle with salt and pepper to taste and Parmesan cheese. Stir to coat.

Vegetable Lo-Mein

1 pkg. lo-mein noodles
1 env. chow mein seasoning mix
1 clove garlic, minced
1 T. minced ginger
1 onion, chopped
3 ribs celery, sliced
1 C. grated carrots
1/2 head cabbage, thinly sliced
2 green onions, chopped

Cook and drain noodles. Prepare seasoning sauce according to package directions. Sauté garlic and ginger in olive oil 30 seconds. Add vegetables and stir-fry until tender. Stir in noodles and sauce. Heat through.

Ham-Fried Rice

2 C. day-old cooked rice
1/4 C. vegetable oil
4 eggs, slightly beaten
1 can chopped ham
1 C. frozen peas and carrots
1 T. soy sauce

Sauté rice in oil until golden brown. Stir in eggs and cook until done. Stir in ham and vegetables. Cover and simmer 30 minutes. Stir in soy sauce. Heat through.

2 boneless chicken breasts, chopped
1 onion, diced
1 bell pepper, diced
2 carrots, diced
1 14.5-oz. can pineapple tidbits
1/4 C. apple cider vinegar
2 T. cornstarch
1/4 C. brown sugar

Stir-fry chicken until tender. Remove from pan. Stir-fry vegetables until tender. Drain pineapple; reserve juice. Stir pineapple juice, vinegar, cornstarch, and brown sugar into vegetables. Cook and stir until thickened. Stir in chicken and pineapple. Serve over rice.

Teriyaki Rice Bowls

2 chicken breast halves, cubed
2 T. sesame oil or vegetable oil
2 C. chopped vegetables (carrots, broccoli, celery, cabbage, etc.)
1 C. teriyaki sauce
1/2 tsp. garlic powder
Green onions, thinly sliced
Sesame seeds (optional)

Stir-fry chicken in hot oil. Remove from pan. Heat sesame oil and sauté vegetables until tender. Stir in teriyaki sauce and garlic powder. Add chicken and stir to coat. Serve over hot rice. Garnish with sliced green onions and sesame seeds. Serve with cooked rice

Orange Rice

1/4 C. butter
1/2 C. chopped celery
1/4 C. chopped green onion
1 C. long-grain rice
1 C. orange juice
1 C. water
1/2 tsp. salt
1 orange, sectioned
1/2 C. slivered almonds

Melt butter in a heavy pot. Sauté celery and onions in butter. Add rice. Sauté until yellow. Add orange juice, water, and salt. Boil. Cover and cook on low 20 minutes or until rice is tender. Add orange sections and almonds just before serving.

Cilantro Lime Rice

2 C. long-grain rice
2 T. butter
2 tsp. chicken bouillon
1 lime, juiced, divided
1 4-oz. can diced green chilis
Handful of fresh cilantro, chopped

Boil 4 C. water in a soup pot. Add rice, butter, bouillon, 1/2 of the lime juice, and green chilis. Cover and cook on low for 20-30 minutes or until tender. Stir in remaining lime juice and fresh, chopped cilantro.

Mexican Rice

6 slices bacon
4 C. water
1 C. salsa
2 C. long-grain rice
1 tsp. salt
1 tsp. chili powder

In a large pot, cook bacon until crisp. Remove bacon and crumble; set aside. Add 4 C. water and salsa to bacon grease. Bring to a boil. Stir in rice, salt, and chili powder. Reduce heat. Cover and simmer 20 minutes. Stir in crumbled bacon during last 5 minutes cooking time.

Baked Spanish Rice

4 slices bacon
1 lb. ground beef
2 C. long-grain rice
1 tsp. chili powder
1 tsp. salt
1 C. salsa
4 C. water
1 C. grated cheddar cheese

Cook bacon and ground beef until done. Drain excess grease. Combine cooked meat with rice, chili powder, salt, and salsa in a 9x13 baking dish. Stir in 4 C. boiling water. Cover with foil and bake 30 minutes. Remove foil; sprinkle with cheese. Bake 15 minutes.

2 eggs
2/3 C. milk
1 C. soft bread crumbs
1 lb. hamburger
1/4 C. chopped onion
2 tsp. baking powder
Salt and pepper to taste
1 can cream of mushroom soup

Blend eggs, milk, and bread crumbs. Combine with hamburger, onion, baking powder, salt, and pepper. Shape into balls. Cook in a skillet until browned. Place meatballs in a baking dish. Combine soup and 1/2 soup can of water with meat drippings. Pour over meatballs. Bake at 350 for 30 minutes. Serve over rice.

Chicken and Rice

2 chicken breasts, cubed
1 C. uncooked long-grain rice
2 cans cream of mushroom soup
1 pkg. dry onion soup mix
3 C. milk

Place chicken in a 9x13 baking dish. Combine remaining ingredients and spread over the chicken. Cover with foil. Bake at 350 for 1 hour. Remove foil. Bake 15 minutes more.

Variations: Stir in 2 C. frozen peas after removing foil. Bake 15 minutes.
Substitute 1 lb. cooked and drained sausage for the chicken.

Creamy Broccoli Rice

- 2 ribs celery, chopped
- 1 onion, chopped
- 2 T. butter
- 2 1/4 C. water
- 2 C. chopped broccoli
- 2 C. long-grain rice
- Salt and pepper to taste
- 1 can cream of mushroom soup
- 1 can cream of chicken soup
- 1 C. grated cheddar cheese
- 1 soup can milk

Sauté celery and onion in butter until soft. Combine with water, broccoli, rice, and salt and pepper in a 9x13 baking dish. Cover with foil. Bake at 350 for 45 minutes. Stir in soups, cheese, and 1 soup can of milk. Cook uncovered 15 minutes.

Tuna and Rice Casserole

- 2 T. butter
- 1 tsp. salt
- 2 C. long-grain rice
- 2 cans tuna, drained
- 1 10-oz. can cream of mushroom soup
- 1 15-oz. can green beans, drained

In a large pot, bring 4 C. water to a boil. Stir in butter, salt, and rice. Reduce temperature to low. Cover and simmer 20 minutes. Stir in tuna, soup, and green beans. Heat through.

Recipes and Notes

Fruits and Vegetables

Nutritional Facts

Adding fruits and vegetables to your menu is essential for a healthy diet. Here is a list of the nutrients contained in these powerful foods.

Vitamin A: An antioxidant, it is mportant for growth and development; immunity; healthy bones, teeth and skin; and good vision.

Good sources of vitamin A are sweet potatoes, carrots, broccoli, kale, spinach. dark leafy greens, winter squash, apricots, cantaloupe, pumpkin, and bell peppers.

B Vitamins: Support cellular energy production and normal nervous system function. Help support cardiovascular (heart) health. Help prevent stomach problems and upper respiratory Illness.

Sources include bananas, bell peppers, broccoli, potatoes, turnip greens, spinach. strawberries, parsley, beets, yams, sweet potatoes, asparagus, peas, and romaine lettuce.

Vitamin C: Supports growth and repair of tissues in all parts of the body. It helps the body make collagen (a protein used to make skin, cartilage, tendons, ligaments, and blood vessels). Needed for healing wounds and repairing and maintaining bones and teeth. It also helps the body absorb iron.

Good sources include apples, Brussels sprouts, cauliflower, cabbage, citrus juices, raw and cooked leafy greens, red and green peppers, potatoes, sweet potatoes, winter squash, zucchini, raspberries, blueberries, cranberries, peas, and pineapple.

Vitamin E: An antioxidant, it helps prevent oxidation of LDL cholesterol, which is needed for structure and maintenance of skeletal, cardiac, and smooth muscle; it also helps form red blood cells.

Sources include avocados, spinach, Swiss chard, beet greens, turnip greens, and kale.

Vitamin K: Needed for the clotting of blood, bone health, and memory.

Try kale, spinach, collards, Swiss chard, broccoli, Brussels sprouts, cabbage, asparagus, and peas.

Vitamin K is higher when these vegetables are cooked.

Calcium: Needed for healthy bones and teeth, helps blood to clot, helps muscles to contract.
Iron: Needed to help build muscles and maintain healthy blood by making the protein called hemoglobin.
Magnesium: Essential in preventing coronary artery spasms (a significant cause of heart attacks).
Manganese: Helps the body form connective tissue, bones, and blood-clotting factors. It also plays a role in fat and carbohydrate metabolism, calcium absorption, and blood sugar regulation. Manganese is necessary for normal brain and nerve function.
Phosphorus: Needed for bones and teeth and for metabolism, which helps utilize carbohydrates, protein, and fat.
Potassium: Helps the nervous system function properly and regulates fluid levels. It is also an electrolyte, a substance that conducts electricity in the body, along with sodium, chloride, calcium, and magnesium. Potassium is crucial to heart function and plays a key role in skeletal and smooth muscle contraction.
Selenium: Increases antioxidant capabilities and the quality of blood flow.
Sodium: Helps control blood pressure and regulates the function of muscles and nerves.
Zinc: Needed for the immune system to work properly. Zinc helps in cell division, cell growth, and wound healing. It is also important for brain function.

Budget-Saving Tip

Adding fruits and vegetables to your menu is not only healthy but it's also a great way to extend your budget . . . especially if you grow a garden! When purchasing produce, you can save money by planning your menu with produce that is in season or during holidays and other times when certain items usually go on sale. Here's what's budget-friendly by season:

Fall: Tomatoes, peppers, peaches, pears, apples, broccoli, potatoes, onions, winter squash.
Winter: Oranges, apples, yams, sweet potatoes, frozen peas, celery, cranberries.
Spring: Strawberries and other berries, asparagus, cabbage, spinach, lettuce.
Summer: Grapes, pineapple, cherries, apricots, melons, tomatoes, peppers, broccoli, lettuce, summer squash, cucumbers, and corn on the cob.

Curry Chicken and Squash

8 cloves garlic, minced
6 green onions, minced
2 T. minced ginger root
2 tsp. dried thyme leaves
2 tsp. ground allspice
1 tsp. ground cloves
1 T. honey
Zest of 2 limes plus juice of 1 lime
3 T. soy sauce
3 lbs. boneless chicken thighs, cut up
2 T. olive oil
1 yellow onion, chopped
2 ribs celery, diced
3-4 C. butternut squash, diced
1 red bell pepper, diced
1 tsp. turmeric
1 tsp. each salt and pepper
1 C. chicken broth
1 T. minced jalapeno pepper
1 C. coconut milk

Combine first 9 ingredients. Add chicken and stir until well coated. Cover and refrigerate 4-8 hours. Heat olive oil over medium heat. Sauté onion, celery, squash, and red pepper until squash starts to brown, 5-8 minutes. Stir in turmeric, salt, and pepper; cook 1 minute. Add chicken and the marinade. Cook, stirring often, 5-6 minutes or until chicken is done on edges. Add chicken broth. Bring to a boil. Reduce heat, cover, and simmer 45 minutes, stirring occasionally. Remove lid and add the jalapeno and coconut milk. Simmer uncovered for 15 minutes. If the curry has too much liquid, mix 1 T. cornstarch with 2 T. water. Pour into curry, stirring constantly until thickened. Serve over rice.

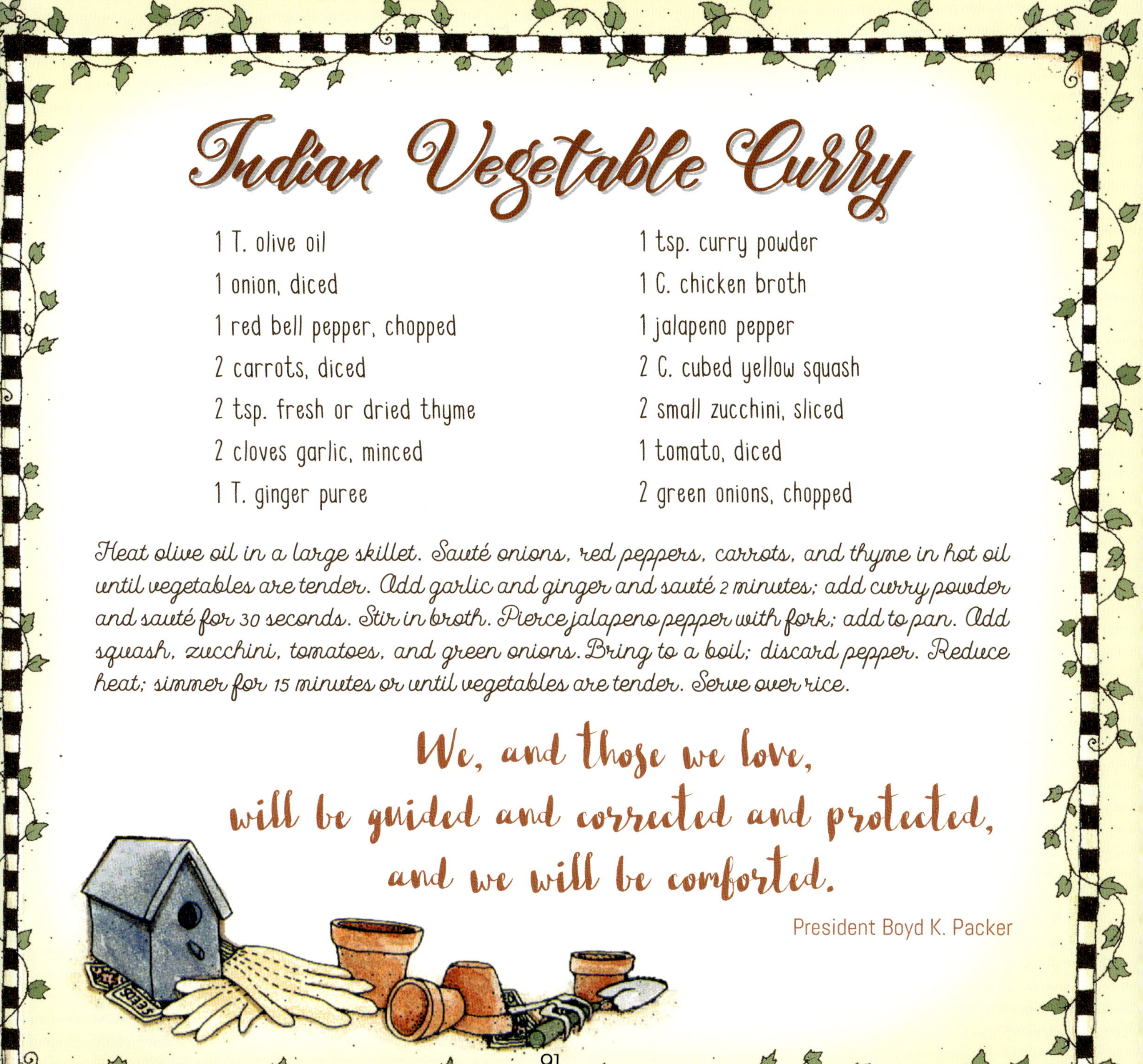

Indian Vegetable Curry

1 T. olive oil
1 onion, diced
1 red bell pepper, chopped
2 carrots, diced
2 tsp. fresh or dried thyme
2 cloves garlic, minced
1 T. ginger puree
1 tsp. curry powder
1 C. chicken broth
1 jalapeno pepper
2 C. cubed yellow squash
2 small zucchini, sliced
1 tomato, diced
2 green onions, chopped

Heat olive oil in a large skillet. Sauté onions, red peppers, carrots, and thyme in hot oil until vegetables are tender. Add garlic and ginger and sauté 2 minutes; add curry powder and sauté for 30 seconds. Stir in broth. Pierce jalapeno pepper with fork; add to pan. Add squash, zucchini, tomatoes, and green onions. Bring to a boil; discard pepper. Reduce heat; simmer for 15 minutes or until vegetables are tender. Serve over rice.

We, and those we love,
will be guided and corrected and protected,
and we will be comforted.

President Boyd K. Packer

Harvest Pumpkin Soup

Sauté 1 onion, finely diced, in 1/4 C. butter until onions begin to brown. Stir in 3 C. pumpkin puree and 3 C. half-and-half. Simmer 10 minutes. Sprinkle with salt and pepper. If desired, remove tops of small individual pumpkins. Scoop out seeds and string pulp. Place pumpkins on individual plates; fill each with creamed soup and replace tops.

You can also make pumpkin bread bowls from recipe in breads section and fill bowls with soup.

Dinner in a Pumpkin

1 medium pumpkin
1 lb. ground beef
1 onion, diced
3 ribs celery, chopped
1 green bell pepper, diced
1 10-oz. can cream of mushroom soup
1/2 soup can of milk
1 15-oz. can green beans, drained
1/4 C. soy sauce
3 C. hot, cooked rice

Wash pumpkin; cut a 4-inch circle around stem. Remove top and set aside. Scoop out seeds and stringy pulp. Place pumpkin on a baking pan; set aside. In a large skillet, cook ground beef, onion, celery, and green pepper over medium heat until meat is no longer pink and vegetables are tender; drain. Stir in the soup, milk, green beans, and soy sauce. Fold in rice; spoon into pumpkin and replace top. Brush outside of pumpkin with oil. Bake at 350 for 50-60 minutes or until pumpkin is just tender. Place on a serving dish. When serving, scoop some of cooked pumpkin onto individual plates along with the rice mixture.

Variations: Add 1 lb. sausage to the ground beef when browning.
Add 1 can mushrooms and 1 can water chestnuts in place of green beans.

Buttered Winter Squash

Cut winter squash in half lengthwise. Place each half cut-side down on a baking sheet. Bake at 425 for 35-45 minutes or until the skin begins to brown and collapse. Remove from oven. Turn squash cut-side up and scoop out flesh. Place in a bowl; add butter, salt, and pepper. Mash with a fork or potato masher until creamy.

Hot Buttered Yams

Peel and chop 3-4 yams and place in a saucepan. Cover with water and sprinkle with salt and pepper. Bring to a boil; reduce heat. Cover and simmer over medium heat 30 minutes or until yams are tender; drain. Return to pan. Add 1 stick butter and mash with a potato masher until smooth and creamy.

Green Bean Yams Casserole

- 3 C. peeled, diced yams
- 1/2 stick butter (1/4 C.)
- 2 15-oz. cans green beans, drained
- 1 10-oz. can cream of mushroom soup
- 1/2 soup can of milk
- 2 C. French-fried onions

Place yams in a lidded saucepan. Cover yams with water and sprinkle with salt and pepper. Bring to a boil; reduce heat. Cover with lid and simmer over medium heat 30 minutes or until yams are tender; drain. Transfer diced yams to a baking dish. Stir in butter and sprinkle with salt and pepper. Fold in drained green beans. Pour soup and milk over top. Sprinkle with French-fried onions. Bake, uncovered, at 350 for 30 minutes.

To make French-fried onions, thinly slice one onion. Dust with flour. Heat oil in a heavy skillet. Place several onions at a time in hot oil. Cook until golden brown. Place on paper towels to absorb grease.

Yummy Yams Casserole

3 C. cooked, buttered yams
3 C. prepared bread stuffing
1 C. cooked, chopped turkey
2 C. turkey gravy

Spread cooked yams in a greased 9x13 baking dish. Spread stuffing over yams. Sprinkle with chopped turkey. Pour gravy over top. Bake at 350 for 30 minutes.

Variation: Substitute chicken meat and gravy for the turkey meat and gravy.

Sweet Potato Skins

4 medium sweet potatoes
1 T. olive oil or melted butter
1/4 C. milk
Salt and pepper to taste
1 C. shredded cheddar cheese
4 strips bacon, cooked and crumbled
Sour cream
Chives or green onions, chopped

Pierce each potato a few times with a fork and place on a baking sheet. Bake at 400 for 40-50 minutes or until soft. Allow potatoes to cool slightly then slice in half lengthwise. Scoop out flesh, leaving a thin layer of sweet potato inside, and place in a bowl. Place skins back on the baking sheet face up; drizzle with olive oil or butter. Reduce oven temperature to 375 and bake skins 10 minutes. Mash sweet potatoes. Stir in milk, salt, andpepper until smooth and creamy. Fill skins with mashed potatoes and top with cheese. Bake 15 minutes or until cheese is melted. Remove from oven and top with bacon, sour cream, and chives.

Kale Sweet Potato Quiche

3 eggs
1 C. grated Parmesan cheese
1/2 C. canola oil
1 T. minced fresh parsley
1 garlic clove, minced
Salt and pepper to taste
1 C. flour
2 tsp. baking powder
1/2 tsp. salt
3 C. sliced zucchini
1 small onion, chopped

In a large bowl, whisk the first six ingredients. In a separate bowl, combine the flour, baking powder, and salt. Stir into the egg mixture. Fold in the zucchini and onion. Pour into a greased 9-inch deep-dish pie plate. Bake at 350 for 25–35 minutes or until lightly browned.

Baked Sweet Potato Fries

1/2 tsp. ground cumin
1/2 tsp. garlic powder
1/2 tsp. ground red pepper
Salt and pepper to taste
3 large sweet potatoes
1 T. vegetable oil

Combine spices and salt and pepper. Set aside. Peel potatoes; cut each in half lengthwise, and cut each half into 6 wedges. In a large bowl, combine potatoes, oil, and spice mixture. Toss until potatoes are evenly coated. Spread potatoes on a greased baking sheet. Bake at 400 for 30 minutes or until edges are crisp and potatoes are cooked through.

Baked Zucchini Fries

1 C. bread crumbs
1/2 C. Parmesan cheese
1 tsp. Italian seasoning
Salt and pepper to taste

4 zucchini, cut into 3-inch strips
1/2 C. all-purpose flour
2 large eggs, well beaten
Fresh parsley (optional)

Combine bread crumbs, Parmesan cheese, Italian seasoning, salt, and pepper. Working in batches, roll zucchini strips in flour, dip into eggs, then coat with bread crumb mixture. Place zucchini strips onto a greased baking sheet. Bake at 425 for 20 minutes, or until golden brown and crisp. Sprinkle with parsley if desired.

Parmesan Zucchini Crisps

Follow recipe for Baked Zucchini Fries, but slice zucchini into 1/4-inch rounds. Coat zucchini rounds as directed for fries. Heat 2 T. oil in a skillet. Cook 5 or 6 zucchini at a time, until golden and crispy, about 1 minute on each side. Place cooked zucchini on paper towels to absorb excess grease. Continue until all zucchini rounds are cooked.

TIP: To make your own fine bread crumbs, toast wheat and/or white bread slices. Using a knife, scrape sides of toast into a bowl. Continue to re-toast and scrape bread until you have used the whole slice of bread.
For croutons, spread butter on bread slices and sprinkle with garlic powder, salt, and pepper. Cut bread into cubes; spread out on baking sheet. Place baking sheet on bottom rack of oven. Broil on low until tops are toasted. Turn off broiler and keep bread in oven several minutes to dry out.

Zucchini Marinara

8 oz. spaghetti noodles
2 T. butter
1 onion, thinly sliced
1 carrot, thinly sliced
4 small zucchini, thinly sliced
3-4 C. marinara sauce, warmed

Cook noodles according to package directions. Drain. Melt butter in a large skillet. Sauté onion, carrot, and zucchini slices until tender. Place sautéed vegetables on idividual servings of spaghetti. Pour warm marinara sauce over tops. Serve with French bread.

Baked Zucchini Pie

3 eggs
1 C. grated Parmesan cheese
1 stick butter, melted (1/2 C.)
1 T. fresh parsley, minced
Salt and pepper to taste
1 C. all-purpose flour
2 tsp. baking powder
1/2 tsp. salt
3 C. zucchini, sliced
1 small onion, chopped

In a large bowl, whisk the first five ingredients. In a separate bowl, sift flour, baking powder, and salt. Stir into egg mixture. Fold in zucchini and onion. Pour into a greased 9-inch deep-dish pie plate. Bake at 350 for 25-35 minutes or until lightly browned.

Zucchini Casserole

4 C. zucchini, chopped
1 yellow onion, diced
2 carrots, peeled and shredded
1/4 C. butter
1 box chicken stuffing mix
1 can cream of chicken soup
1 C. sour cream
1 C. shredded cheddar cheese

Place vegetables in a soup pot. Pour 2 C. water in pot and sprinkle vegetables with salt and pepper. Bring vegetables to a boil. Reduce temperature; cover and simmer 10 minutes. Drain vegetables; reserve 2 C. liquid. Return 2 C. liquid to pot. Add butter. Bring to a boil. Stir in stuffing mix and remove from heat. Meanwhile combine vegetables with soup, sour cream, and cheese in a 9x13 baking dish. Top with stuffing. Bake at 350 for 30 minutes.

Summer Squash Parmesan

2 C. bow-tie pasta
3 small zucchini, diced
2 small yellow squash, diced
1 T. fresh parsley, chopped
1 T. fresh basil, chopped
1/2 tsp. fresh thyme
1/2 tsp. fresh oregano, chopped
Salt and pepper to taste
1/2 C. grated Parmesan cheese

Cook pasta according to package directions. Drain and spread in a greased 9x13 baking dish. Steam zucchini and yellow squash until just tender. Toss with seasonings. Spread over noodles. Sprinkle with Parmesan cheese. Bake at 350 for 20 minutes.

Hot Steamed Spinach

5-6 C. fresh spinach, chopped
Salt and pepper to taste

Place chopped spinach in a large pot. Add 1 C. water; sprinkle with salt and pepper. Cover and simmer on low 7-8 minutes or until spinach has darkened in color and leaves are limp. Drain. Serve with any meat and/or potato, pasta, or rice dish.

Variation: Stir in 2 T. vinegar while cooking.
Add 1/4 C. hot crumbled bacon to drained spinach.

Spinach Enchiladas

4-5 C. fresh spinach, chopped
1 onion, finely diced
1 jalepeno, seeded and chopped
1 16-oz. container cottage cheese
2 C. shredded cheddar cheese, divided
10 8-inch flour tortillas
1 28-oz. can green enchilada sauce
1 lime, juiced

Steam spinach until tender; drain. Combine spinach with onion, jalepeno, cottage cheese, and 1 C. shredded cheese. Place a heaping spoonful of filling down center of each tortilla. Roll up and place in 9x13 baking dish. Pour enchilada sauce over top and sprinkle with remaining cheese. Bake at 350 for 30 minutes. Drizzle with lime juice when serving.

Variation: Substitute 2-3 C. chopped zucchini for the spinach in this recipe. Sauté zucchini with onion and jalepeno in hot oil or butter until tender. Replace cottage cheese with 1 C. sour cream. Prepare and bake as directed.

Creamy Spinach Penne

2 T. butter
1 tsp. garlic powder
1 C. half-and-half
3 C. fresh spinach, finely chopped
1 C. shredded mozzarella cheese
12-oz. pkg. penne pasta, cooked

Melt butter in a large pot. Add garlic powder; cook 30 seconds. Stir in half-and-half and spinach. Cook until spinach wilts. Add cheese and cook until cheese is melted. Remove from heat. Stir in pasta until well coated and pasta absorbs sauce. Season with salt and pepper if desired. Serve immediately.

Variation: Replace cooked pasta with 3 C. cooked rice. Follow recipe as directed.

Spinach Zucchini Quiche

Pie crust
4 large eggs
1/2 C. milk
Salt and pepper to taste
2 T. butter
1 C, zucchini, shredded
2 C. fresh spinach, chopped
1 C. shredded sharp cheese

Press pie crust into a greased 9x13 baking dish. Whisk eggs, milk, salt, and pepper. Pour into baking dish. Heat butter in a skillet. Sauté zucchini in hot butter until tender. Fold spinach and zucchini into egg mixture. Sprinkle with cheese. Bake at 400 for 30-35 minutes or until edges start to brown and it is firm at center.

Summer Spaghetti

12-oz. pkg. spaghetti noodles
3 cloves garlic, minced
2 T. butter
4 small zucchini, chopped
8-10 garden tomatoes, chopped
1 C. chopped green onions
Fresh basil leaves, chopped
1 C. shredded mozzarella cheese

Cook pasta according to package directions. Meanwhile, sauté garlic in butter 1 minute or until fragrant. Add zucchini and stir-fry 4-5 minutes or until crisp-tender. Stir in chopped tomatoes and green onions. Heat through. Fold in cooked noodles, chopped basil, and mozzarella cheese. Serve warm with garlic French bread.

Hawaiian Haystacks

4 C. hot cooked rice
Chow mein noodles
Chicken gravy (see page 11)
1-2 C. shredded cheddar cheese
Green peas, steamed
Ripe tomatoes, diced
Yellow and/or green onions, diced
Green bell peppers, diced
Black olives, sliced
Fresh or canned pineapple chunks
Mandarin oranges
Flaked coconut

Prepare all ingredients and place in bowls to serve family or buffet style. Allow family members to build their individual haystacks.

Summer Squash Stir-Fry

1 medium onion, cut into thin wedges
1 bell pepper, sliced
2 cloves garlic, minced
2 tsp. ginger root, finely chopped
1 C. chicken broth, divided
3 T. soy sauce
1 T. sugar
1 stalk broccoli, chopped
3 summer squash, sliced
2 tsp. cornstarch

Stir-fry onion, pepper, garlic, and ginger root in small amount of oil until garlic becomes fragrant. Add 3/4 C. broth, soy sauce, and sugar. Cover and cook over medium heat 5 minutes, stirring occasionally. Stir in broccoli and summer squash. Cover and cook about 5 minutes, stirring occasionally, until vegetables are crisp-tender. Combine cornstarch and remaining 1/4 cup broth; stir into vegetables. Cook and stir until sauce is thickened. Serve over cooked rice or noodles.

Zucchini Omelets

2 small zucchini, thinly sliced or shredded
1/4 C, onion, finely diced
2 T. butter
6 eggs, well beaten
1/4 C. milk
1/2 C. shredded cheddar cheese, divided

Sauté zucchini and onion in butter until zucchini begins to brown. In a bowl, whisk eggs and milk. Pour eggs into greased skillet. Sprinkle with 1/4 zucchini mixture, 2 T. cheese, and salt and pepper. Cook until edges are firm; flip and cook other side. Repeat process.

Summer Tacos

1 onion, sliced thin
1 bell pepper, sliced thin
2 zucchini, sliced thin
2 T. vegetable oil
2 C. cooked pinto or black beans
10 corn or flour tortillas
1 C. shredded cheddar cheese
Sour cream
Spinach or lettuce leaves
6-8 tomatoes, chopped
Fresh cilantro
Juice from 1 lime

Sauté onion, pepper, and zucchini in hot oil until vegetables are tender. Fold in beans and warm through. Meanwhile, place a couple of tortillas at a time on a baking sheet. Spread shredded cheese evenly on tortillas. Place on top oven rack and broil on high 2 minutes or until cheese is melted and bubbly.

Spread sour cream over melted cheese, followed by sautéed veggies, spinach or lettuce, tomatoes, cilantro, and lime juice. Roll up and serve warm.

Tomatillo Ranch Dressing

2-3 tomatillos, coarsely chopped
1 small jalapeno, seeded and chopped
1 C. mayonnaise
1 C. buttermilk
1/2 env. ranch dressing mix
4-5 sprigs fresh cilantro
Juice from 1 lime

Place all ingredients in a blender. Puree until smooth. Allow to sit at least 15 minutes before serving.

Fresh Tomato Salsa

8-10 Roma tomatoes, diced
Garlic powder, salt, and pepper
1 yellow onion, finely diced
1 C. green bell pepper, finely diced
1 small jalapeno pepper, finely diced (optional)
1/2 C. cilantro leaves, minced (optional)
Juice from 1 lime (optional)

Place tomatoes in serving bowl. Sprinkle with generous amounts of garlic powder, salt, and pepper. Allow to meld while cutting onions and peppers. Stir in remaining ingredients. This salsa may be served fresh or stored overnight in refrigerator. If storing overnight, add cilantro or lime juice just before serving.

Oven-Roasted Green Beans

1 lb. green beans, washed and trimmed
1/4 C. butter, thinly sliced
Salt and pepper to taste
2 T. dried onion flakes

Place washed and trimmed green beans in a buttered 9x13 baking dish. Place butter slices on green beans and sprinkle with salt, pepper, and onion flakes. Bake at 425 for 20-25 minutes or until beans are slightly shriveled and have brown spots.

Variations: Cook and crumble 6 slices bacon. Stir in bacon last 10 minutes of cooking time. Sprinkle with 1/2 C. grated Parmesan cheese after sprinkling with onion flakes.

Aunt Lila's Creamed Peas

1 lb. fresh or frozen peas
1/4 C. butter
1/4 C. all-purpose flour
3 C. milk
Salt and pepper to taste

Steam peas until tender. Meanwhile, melt butter in a large skillet; stir in flour until it forms a paste. Slowly stir in milk. Cook and stir until thickened and bubbly. Sprinkle with salt and a generous amount of black pepper. Drain peas; fold into creamed mixture.

Creamy Asparagus

Steam asparagus with salt and pepper until tender. Serve with white sauce or cheese sauce from opposite page drizzled over individual servings.

Broccoli and Cheese Sauce

3 stalks broccoli, chopped
Salt and pepper to taste
3 C. white sauce
1 1/2 C. shredded cheddar cheese

Place chopped broccoli in a large sauce pan. Add 1 C. water. Sprinkle with salt and pepper. Cover and simmer on medium-low 8-10 minutes or until broccoli is tender. Meanwhile, prepare white sauce from Creamed Peas recipe on opposite page. Stir in shredded cheese until melted. Drizzle cheese sauce over individual servings of steamed broccoli.

Broccoli Stir-fry

1 T. fresh ginger, grated
1 T. vegetable oil
2 carrots, peeled and thinly sliced
1 bunch green onions, chopped
6 C. broccoli, cut into florets
1 bell pepper, chopped
1/4 C. hoisin sauce
1/2 C. water
1 T. sesame seeds
Cooked rice

In a large skillet, cook ginger in hot oil until fragrant, about 30 seconds. Add carrots, green onions, broccoli, and bell pepper. Stir-fry 3-5 minutes or until broccoli is crisp-tender. Add hoisin sauce and 1/2 C. water. Simmer until broccoli is tender. Sprinkle with sesame seeds. Serve over hot cooked rice.

Cabbage Egg Rolls

1/2 lb. bulk pork sausage
3 carrots, peeled and shredded
1/2 onion, diced
1/2 cabbage head, chopped
3-4 garlic cloves, minced
1 T. fresh ginger, minced
1/4 C. cilantro, chopped
Salt and pepper to taste
16 egg roll wrappers
Oil for frying

Cook sausage in a large skillet until no longer pink. Add carrots, onions, and cabbage; stir-fry until carrots are tender. Add garlic and ginger; stir-fry 1 minute. Stir in cilantro, salt, and pepper. Place 3 T. filling at one corner of egg roll wrapper. Fold up corner then both sides as you would for a burrito and roll up. Dip your finger in water and run it along remaining corner of the wrapper. Press down to seal. Repeat with remaining wrappers. Cook 4-5 egg rolls at a time in hot oil until golden. Flip and cook until golden brown. Transfer to a dish lined with paper towels to absorb excess grease before serving.

Cabbage Potstickers

Follow recipe for Cabbage Egg Rolls but replace egg roll wrappers with wonton wrappers. Place 1 T. filling in the center of wonton wrapper. Dip your finger in water and run it along the entire edge of the wrapper. Fold both ends up to make a triangle and lightly pinch together, making sure the potsticker is sealed. Drop several potstickers at a time into boiling water. Boil 5 minutes; drain. Pour just enough oil to coat the bottom of a skillet. Cook 4-5 potstickers at a time 2 minutes or until crisp and golden. Flip and cook another 2 minutes.

Green Tomato Salsa

4 green tomatoes, quartered
4 ripe tomatoes, quartered
1 onion, quartered
3-4 garlic cloves
1-2 jalapeno peppers, seeded and chopped
1/2 C. fresh cilantro, chopped
1 tsp. red curry powder
1 tsp. oregano powder
Salt and pepper to taste
Juice of 2 limes

Place ingredients in order in a food processor or blender. Pulse until well blended. Serve with Cabbage Egg Rolls.

Potsticker Dipping Sauce

1/4 C. green onions, finely chopped
1/4 C. sesame oil
2 T. sugar
1/4 C. soy sauce
1/4 C. vinegar
1/4 C. water
1/4 tsp. crushed red pepper

Sauté green onions in sesame oil 1 minute. Stir in remaining ingredients. Cook and stir until sugar is dissolved, about 1 minute. Cool. Serve with Cabbage Potstickers

You can add any garden vegetables to these egg rolls or potstickers. We like to make them at the end of summer to use the unripened tomatoes for Green Tomato Salsa.

Spinach and Broccoli Salad

6 slices bacon, cooked and crumbled
1 pkg. baby spinach
2 C. broccoli, chopped
1 C. dried cranberries
3 stems green onions, chopped
8 oz. sunflower seeds (optional)

Combine all ingredients. Serve with Poppy Seed Dressing (below), pouring dressing over salad just before serving.

Poppy Seed Dressing

3/4 C. grape juice
1/4 C. apple cider vinegar
1/2 C. oil
2 tsp. dry mustard
1/4 C. sugar
1 tsp. salt
2-3 T. poppy seeds

Combine all ingredients in a blender.

Dried Cranberries

Dump a 12-oz. bag of cranberries into a bowl; pour boiling water over top. Allow to sit in the water until the skin pops. Drain. Coat berries with 1/4 C. sugar. Transfer to a baking sheet and place in a freezer for 2 hours. Heat oven to 350. Keep heated for 10 minutes. Turn oven off and place cranberries in oven. Keep in oven 8 hours or overnight.

Bacon Broccoli Salad

10 bacon strips, cooked and crumbled
2 large broccoli stalks, chopped
1 red onion, diced
1/2 C. shredded cheddar cheese
1 C. dried cranberries
1 C. mayonnaise
1 C. sour cream
1/4 C. sugar
1/4 C. apple cider vinegar
1 C. cashew nuts

Combine crumbled bacon, broccoli, onion, cheese, and cranberries. Stir mayonnaise, sour cream, sugar, and vinegar into salad. Add nuts 1/2 hour before serving.

BLT Pasta Salad

1/2 C. plain yogurt or sour cream
1/2 C. mayonnaise
16 oz. macaroni
10 slices bacon, cooked and crumbled
2 C. grape tomatoes, quartered
Salt and pepper to taste
2 C. romaine lettuce, chopped

Combine yogurt and mayonnaise to make dressing; set aside. Cook pasta; drain. Combine pasta with bacon and tomatoes. Season with salt and pepper. Add lettuce and dressing just before serving.

Variations: Add 1 C. cubed mozzarella, cheddar, or Swiss cheese.
Replace 1 C. chopped romaine lettuce with spinach leaves.
Add 2–3 stems green onions, chopped.

1 chicken breast, cooked and cubed
1/2 C. mayonnaise
1/2 C. sour cream
1 onion, finely diced
3 celery ribs, diced
2 C. red grapes, halved
1 C. pineapple tidbits (optional)
Salt and pepper to taste
Pita bread (can use tortillas, rolls, or bread)
Sprouts (optional)

Stir first 8 ingredients until well combined using a generous amount of pepper. Cut pita bread pieces in half. Stuff chicken salad into pita pockets. If desired, top with sprouts.

Chicken Pasta Salad

1 8-oz. pkg. bow-tie pasta
1 15-oz. can pineapple tidbits, drained
1 C. salad dressing
1 T. apple cider vinegar
3 T. sugar
Salt and pepper to taste
1 onion, finely diced
3 celery ribs, diced
2 C. red grapes, halved
1 chicken breast, cooked and cubed

Cook pasta according to package directions. Cool completely. Put pineapple in a strainer or sieve to drain thoroughly. Combine salad dressing, vinegar, sugar, and salt and pepper. Fold in remaining ingredients. Chill 30 minutes before serving.

Greek Pasta Salad

1 12-oz. pkg. rainbow rotelli pasta
1 C. cottage cheese
1 8-oz. bottle Italian dressing
1 T. dill weed
4 tsp. dried parsley
1 15-oz. can kidney beans, drained
1 red onion, diced
2 cucumbers, chopped
2 C. grape tomatoes, halved
1 6-oz. can black olives, sliced

Cook pasta according to package directions. In a large bowl, combine cottage cheese, dressing, dill weed, and parsley. Fold in pasta and remaining ingredients. Chill for 30 minutes before serving.

Easy Peasy Tuna Salad

1 16-oz. pkg. seashell pasta
1 C. Miracle Whip
1 6-oz. jar dill pickle relish
1/2 C. finely diced onion
2 cans tuna fish, drained
1 6-oz. can ripe olives, sliced
2 C. grape tomatoes, halved (optional)
2 C. frozen peas, thawed

Cook pasta according to package directions. Drain pasta and cool completely. In a separate bowl, combine salad dressing, relish, and diced onion. Sprinkle with salt and pepper. Fold in pasta, tuna, sliced olives, tomatoes, and peas.

TIP: After chopping green onions, place the onion bulb in a glass of 3-4 inches of water. It will grow new green tops within a few days. Do this several times to extend use of the onion.

Creamy Cucumber Salad

1/2 C. mayonnaise
1/2 C. sour cream
1/4 C. sugar
2 T. distilled white vinegar
3 tsp. dried dill weed
Salt and pepper to taste
4 cucumbers, peeled and thinly sliced
1 red onion, thinly sliced

Combine first 6 ingredients; stir until well blended. Fold in cucumbers and onion. Chill for 30 minutes before serving.

Layered Lettuce Salad

1 head romaine lettuce, chopped
4 hard-cooked eggs, sliced
2 large tomatoes, chopped
2 C. frozen peas, patted dry
6 bacon strips, cooked and crumbled
1 C. shredded cheddar cheese
1 red onion, thinly sliced
1 1/2 C. mayonnaise
1/2 C. sour cream
1 tsp. dill weed
3/4 tsp. dried basil
1/2 tsp. salt
1/8 tsp. pepper
Fresh dill sprigs, optional

In a deep trifle bowl, layer in order: lettuce, eggs, tomatoes, peas, bacon, cheese, and onion. In a small bowl, combine mayonnaise, sour cream, dill, basil, salt, and pepper. Spread on top of salad. Cover and refrigerate for several hours or overnight. Garnish with fresh dill sprigs if desired.

Favorite Sarah Salad

1 head Romaine lettuce, chopped
2 C. frozen peas
1 purple onion, diced
4 oz. mozzarella cheese, cubed
1/2 C. mayonnaise
1/4 C. granulated sugar
Salt and pepper to taste
4 strips bacon, cooked and crumbled

Toss vegetables and cheese in a large bowl. In a small bowl, blend mayonnaise, sugar, salt, and pepper. Stir dressing and bacon into salad just before serving.

Recipes and Notes

Breads and Grains

Using bread and grains is a great way to stretch food dollars, but you need to be wise because it is also a one of the easiest ways to blow the food budget. Although you can bake your own bread and bakery items for about $.50 a pound, buying commercial baked goods costs between $1.50 and $7.00 per pound. Because baked items smell so good when you enter the grocery store and because they are so convenient, it is next to impossible to not give in to these purchases. But let me give you a little rundown of the costs. On the low end, dinner rolls cost about $2.50 a dozen (fresh, not the day-old from discount bread stores that are really two weeks old). If you spend $2.50 for one pound of rolls once a week, that is $1.50 excess. You likely buy 2 loaves of bread per week. If it's wheat bread, you pay at least $2.50 a loaf compared to the $.50 it costs to bake a loaf. That is $4.00 a week excess. A package of tortillas at $1.50 is an excess of $1.20. What about the refrigerator biscuits and freezer rolls? And the the bisquick, pancake mix, cornbread, and muffin mixes you have in the pantry? They cost between $1.15 and $1.50 per pound compared to making your own for $.32 to $.50 per pound. Even if you only use those mixes twice in a week, that is an excess of $2.00. Basically, each time you purchase a bread product rather than bake, you spend about $2.00 more. That doesn't seem like much, does it? After all, it's only $2.00. But when you add up those dollars, it makes a big difference. Even if your family only consumes 1 pound of bread per day, that is $60.00 a month excess. And my calculations were for the low end. The average is much higher.

The purpose of this section is to show that a big portion of the food budget can be saved by baking your own bread and bread products. And because of electric mixers, it doesn't take very much time. But most importantly, your family will love you for it! Nothing compares to fresh, home-baked bread!

This section also includes ideas for using grains to stretch the meat in your meals.

Nutritional Facts

Not only will you save money by baking your own bread products, but they are more nutritious as well. Of course, I am talking about whole-grain products, but even white bread baked at home is better for you than what you buy at the store because homemade is free of preservatives. Here are some nutritional facts:

Percentage of daily nutrients in a serving of hard red wheat: 31% protein, 22% fiber, 8% carbohydrate, 12% thiamin, 8% riboflavin, 16% niacin, 8% folic acid, 8% calcium, 12% iron, 36% manganese, 10% copper, 10% magnesium, and 8% pantothenic acid.

Percentage of daily nutrients in a serving of rolled oats: 13% protein, 17% fiber, 125% vitamin B, 21% iron, 96% manganese, 64% molybdenum, 29% phosphorus, 27% copper, 26% biotin, 17% magnesium, 15% chromium, and 14% zinc.

Extensive research suggests regular consumption of whole grains (especially whole wheat) is linked to a lower risk of high blood pressure, heart disease, heart attack, and certain cancers. Eating whole grains also reduces the risk of type 2 diabetes.

Budget-Saving Tip

Purchase a bread machine instead of a more expensive mixer. Use the dough setting for kneading and raising the dough, but bake your bread in the oven. I paid $39 for my bread machine and have used it as a mixer for nearly twenty years . . . and it is still going strong! My daughter bought one at a yard sale and the heating element was broken, but it still works great as a mixer.

Fresh-Baked Bread

2/3 C. sugar
2 C. warm water
1 1/2 T. active dry yeast
1/4 C. nonfat dry milk (optional)
1 1/2 tsp. salt
1/4 C. vegetable oil
6 C. bread flour

In a large bowl or mixer, dissolve sugar in warm water; stir in yeast. Allow to sit until yeast resembles a creamy foam. Mix dry milk, salt, and oil into the yeast. Mix in flour one cup at a time. Knead dough on a lightly floured surface until smooth. Place in a well-oiled bowl and turn dough to coat. Cover with a damp cloth. Allow to rise until doubled in bulk, about 1 hour. Punch dough down. Knead for a few minutes and divide in half. Shape into 2 loaves and place into two well-oiled 9x5 loaf pans. Let rise in a warm area 30 minutes, or until dough has risen 1 inch above pans. Bake at 350 for 30 minutes. Remove from oven and turn onto a rack to cool. If desired, rub crust with butter. Cool completely before slicing. Store in a plastic bag after bread is completely cooled.

Creamy Honey Butter

1 stick butter, softened
1/2 C. honey
1/2 C. powdered sugar
1/2 tsp. vanilla

Whip all ingredients together until creamy and fluffy. Serve with warm bread or scones.

Deep-Fried Scones

Follow recipe for whole-wheat or white bread. Allow dough to raise 45 minutes to 1 hour. Divide dough into 2-inch balls. Stretch or roll balls to 1/4-inch thickness. Fry in hot oil on both sides. Place on paper towels to drain excess oil. Serve with soups or stews, as a treat with fresh jam or honey butter, or use for Navajo Tacos.

Whole-Wheat Bread

- 1 T. active dry yeast
- 1 C. lukewarm water
- 1/4 C. honey or molasses
- 1/4 C. vegetable oil
- 1 1/4 tsp. salt
- 3 1/3 C. whole-wheat flour

In a large bowl or mixer, dissolve yeast in water. Add remaining ingredients and stir until the dough forms a ball. Transfer to a lightly floured surface; knead 6-8 minutes (or knead dough in a mixer), until dough becomes smooth. Note: Dough should be soft, yet still firm enough to knead. Adjust consistency with additional water or flour if necessary. Place dough in a lightly greased bowl. Cover and let rise in a warm area until puffy (about 1 hour). Punch dough down; shape into an 8-inch log, place in a lightly greased loaf pan, and cover loosely with lightly greased plastic wrap. Let rise until center is 1 inch above pan (about 1 hour). Bake at 350 for 35-40 minutes or until browned and bread makes a hollow sound when thumped on top. Remove from oven and turn onto a rack to cool. If desired, rub crust with butter. Cool completely before slicing.

Heavenly Dinner Rolls

1 T. yeast
1 C. warm water
1 stick butter
1 C. milk
2 eggs
1/3 C. sugar
1 T. salt
4-5 C. flour

In a large bowl or mixer, dissolve yeast in water, Melt butter in a saucepan. Stir in milk until just warm. Add milk mixtue and remaining ingredients to dissolved yeast. Knead dough in mixer or by hand 5-7 minutes or until dough is smooth and elastic. Let rest 10 minutes. Place dough on lightly floured surface. Turn once. Divide in half. Roll each half into a circle with a thickness of about 1/2 inch. Cut circle, as you would a pizza, into 8-12 wedges. Starting at the widest part of wedge, roll up and secure tip with a dab of water. Shape into crescents as you place them on a greased baking sheet. Repeat with remaining dough. Cover and let rise in warm area 30 minutes. Bake at 350 for 20-22 minutes or until golden brown.

Freezer Dinner Rolls

Follow recipe for dough from Heavenly or Quick Dinner Rolls. After shaping dough into 1-inch balls or crescent rolls, dust them lightly with flour and place them on an ungreased baking sheet. Place baking sheet in freezer for 1 hour. Put frozen rolls in large zip-top bag. Return to freezer. When cooking, remove frozen rolls from bag and place on a greased baking sheet. Cover and put in a warm place to thaw and rise (about 2 hours). Bake at 350 for 20-22 minutes or until golden brown.

Quick Dinner Rolls

2 1/2 C. warm water
1/3 C. sugar
1/4 C. oil
1 T. salt
1 egg
1/4 C. nonfat dry milk
1 1/4 T. yeast
4-5 C. flour

In a mixer, combine all ingredients except flour. Mix 8 minutes while gradually adding enough flour to make a workable dough that is still sticky. Let rest 8 minutes. Place dough on lightly floured surface. Turn once. Shape dough into 1-inch balls. Place on greased baking sheet. Cover and let rise in warm area 20 minutes. Bake at 350 for 22 minutes.

Buttery Breadsticks

2 tsp. active dry yeast
1 1/3 C. warm water
1/4 C. vegetable oil
2 T. sugar
1 tsp. salt
4 C. wheat or white flour
1 stick butter, softened

In a large bowl or mixer, dissolve yeast in water, Add remaining ingredients. Knead dough in mixer or by hand 5-7 minutes or until dough is smooth and elastic. Spread dough entirely to edges of greased sheet cake pan. Spread softened butter on top of dough. Using a pizza cutter, slice breadsticks 1 inch wide. Let rise 15-20 minutes. Bake at 350 for 30 minutes or until golden brown. Serve with soups and stews.

Bread Bowls

Make recipe for Quick Dinner Rolls. Divide dough into 8 parts. Form into balls and place on greased baking sheets sprinkled with cornmeal. Cover and let rise until double. Bake at 375 for 25 minutes. Cool and cut off tops. Scoop out bread to make bowls.

Pumpkin Bread Bowls

For a fun fall treat, make your bread bowls (see recipe above) to look like little pumpkins. Squirt 2–3 drops each of red and yellow food coloring into warm water (until it is a deep orange) before making the bread dough. Divide dough into 8 parts. Pinch one tiny ball off each part for the stem. Roll the 8 parts into balls and place them on a greased baking pan. Press a knife blade through top of balls several times as you would to cut a pie, making sure to cut into the dough; these will be the lines on the pumpkins. Place a few drops of green food coloring in 1/4 C. water. Roll each of the pinched-off pieces into a log and dip in green food coloring. Press into top of ball to be the stem. Continue as directed.

Love one another as I have loved you.

John 13:34

Ham 'n Cheese Hot Pockets

Quick Dinner Rolls dough
2 C. shredded cheddar cheese
1/2 lb. sliced ham, chopped
Butter, softened (optional)

Roll dough very thin (as you would for pizza crust) into a large rectangle. Place on a well-greased baking sheet with half of the dough on the pan. Spread butter, if desired, over the dough on the pan. Layer with chopped ham and shredded cheese. Fold other half of dough over toppings. Cut into 1x4-inch pieces; using the tines of a fork, press down around all of the edges to seal. Bake at 450 for 10-12 minutes or until golden brown.

Creamy Chicken Roll-ups

Heavenly Dinner Rolls dough
8-oz. cream cheese, softened
2 C. chopped cooked chicken
Grated Parmesan cheese
1 env. chicken gravy mix
1 C. milk

Divide dough in half. Roll each half into a circle with a thickness of about 1/2 inch. Spread cream cheese over dough; sprinkle chopped chicken and Parmesan cheese over top. Cut circle, as you would a pizza, into 8-12 wedges. Starting at the widest part of wedge, roll up and secure tip with a toothpick. Shape into crescents as you place them on a greased baking sheet. Repeat with remaining dough. Cover and let rise in warm area 15-20 minutes. Bake at 350 for 20-22 minutes or until golden brown. Make gravy according to package directions; drizzle over chicken roll-ups when serving.

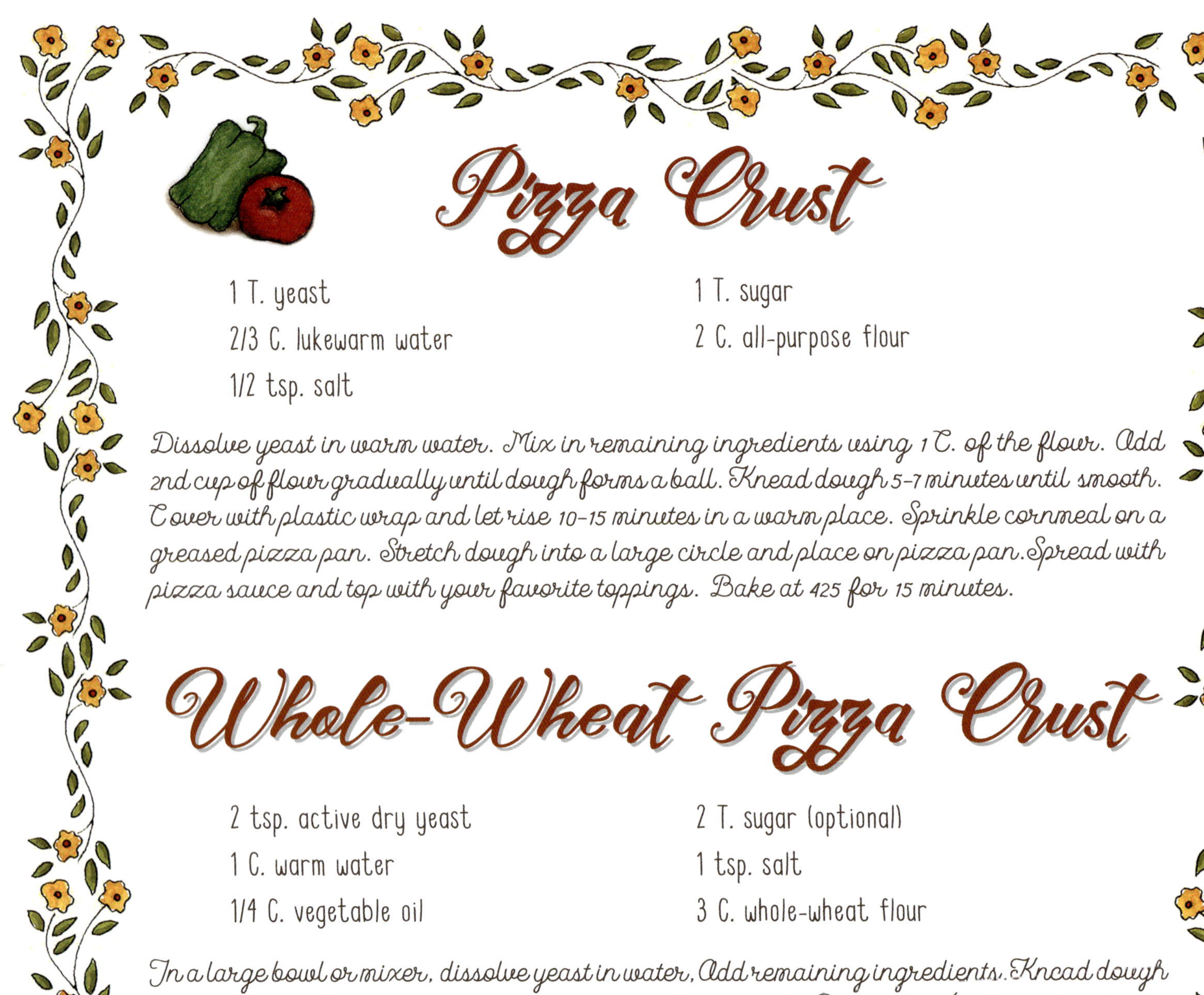

Pizza Crust

1 T. yeast
2/3 C. lukewarm water
1/2 tsp. salt
1 T. sugar
2 C. all-purpose flour

Dissolve yeast in warm water. Mix in remaining ingredients using 1 C. of the flour. Add 2nd cup of flour gradually until dough forms a ball. Knead dough 5-7 minutes until smooth. Cover with plastic wrap and let rise 10-15 minutes in a warm place. Sprinkle cornmeal on a greased pizza pan. Stretch dough into a large circle and place on pizza pan. Spread with pizza sauce and top with your favorite toppings. Bake at 425 for 15 minutes.

Whole-Wheat Pizza Crust

2 tsp. active dry yeast
1 C. warm water
1/4 C. vegetable oil
2 T. sugar (optional)
1 tsp. salt
3 C. whole-wheat flour

In a large bowl or mixer, dissolve yeast in water, Add remaining ingredients. Knead dough in mixer or by hand 5-7 minutes, or until dough is smooth. Pinch off 1/3 of the dough; set aside. Sprinkle cornmeal on a greased pizza pan. Stretch remaining dough into large circle and place on pizza pan. Bake at 425 for 15 minutes. Cool slightly. Spread with pizza sauce and top with your favorite toppings. Bake at 425 an additional 10-15 minutes or until cheese is bubbly and beginning to brown. Use remaining dough for breadsticks.

Quick and Easy Pizza Sauce

- 1 15-oz. can crushed tomatoes
- 1 tsp. garlic powder
- 2 tsp. Italian seasoning
- 2 T. sugar

Combine all ingredients in a saucepan. Simmer until sauce begins to darken in color.

Pizza Pockets

- Quick Dinner Rolls dough
- 2 C. spaghetti sauce
- 2 C. shredded mozzarella cheese
- Pepperoni slices

Roll dough very thin into a large rectangle. Place on a well-greased baking sheet with half of the dough on the pan and the other half off the pan. Spread spaghetti sauce over the dough on the pan. Layer with pepperoni slices and shredded cheese. Fold other half of dough over toppings. Cut into 1x4-inch pieces; using the tines of a fork, press down around all of the edges to seal pockets. Bake at 450 for 10-12 minutes or until golden brown on top.

Buttermilk Biscuits

2 C. flour
4 tsp. baking powder
3 T. sugar
1/2 tsp. salt
1/2 C. butter or shortening
2/3 C. milk

Combine dry ingredients. Cut in butter or shortening until mixture is crumbly. Stir milk into crumb mixture until just moistened. Drop onto pan or roll and cut biscuits and place on lightly greased baking sheet. Bake at 450 for 8-10 minutes.

Creamy Chicken Dumplings

2 C. chopped, cooked chicken, divided
1 can cream of chicken soup
1 soup can of milk
1 recipe Buttermilk Biscuit dough
1/2 C. chopped green onions
2 C. shredded cheddar cheese (optional)

In a large skillet, combine 1 C. chicken with soup and milk. Roll dough into a rectangle of 1/4 inch thickness. Sprinkle remaining chicken, green onions, and shredded cheese over the biscuit dough. Roll dough up jelly-roll style. Slice into 1/2-inch-thick pieces as you would for cinnamon rolls. Bring soup mixture to a boil. Place chicken rolls in soup mixture. Spoon some of the soup mixture over tops of chicken rolls. Reduce to medium-low temperature. Cover skillet and simmer 12-15 minutes or until biscuits are cooked through.

Ham 'n Cheese Biscuit Bites

1 recipe Buttermilk Biscuit dough
2 C. shredded cheddar cheese
1/2 lb. sliced ham
1/2 C. chopped green onions (optional)

Roll dough into a square of 1/4-inch thickness. Spread shredded cheese, sliced ham, and green onions (if desired) over half of the biscuit dough. Fold other half over toppings. Cut into bite-size pieces and place on a lightly greased baking sheet. Bake at 450 for 10–12 minutes or until golden brown on top.

Biscuit Hot Pockets

1 recipe Buttermilk Biscuit dough
2 C. spaghetti sauce
2 C. shredded mozzarella cheese
Pepperoni slices

Roll biscuit dough into a square of 1/4-inch thickness. Spread spaghetti sauce, cheese, and pepperoni slices over half of the biscuit dough. Fold other half over toppings. Cut into bite-size pieces and place on a lightly greased baking sheet. Bake at 450 for 10–12 minutes or until golden brown on top.

Pigs in Blankets

Roll biscuit dough into a square of 1/4-inch thickness. Cut into 3x6-inch pieces. Place a hot dog lengthwise on each piece and roll up. Pinch dough at seam to secure. Bake as above.

Quick and Easy Biscuit Mix

- 9 C. all-purpose or wheat flour
- 1 1/2 C. powdered milk
- 7 T. baking powder
- 1/2 C. sugar
- 4 tsp. salt
- 2 C. shortening or coconut oil

Sift dry ingredients. Cut in shortening or coconut oil until well blended. Place in a sturdy plastic or glass storage container. Cover until ready to use.

Cheeseburger Pie

- 1 lb. lean ground beef
- 1 onion, diced (optional)
- 1 C. shredded Cheddar cheese
- 1 1/2 C. biscuit mix
- 1 C. milk
- 2 eggs

Brown ground beef with onion; drain fat. Spread in a pie plate. Sprinkle with shredded cheese. Combine biscuit mix, milk, and eggs; spoon over top. Bake at 400 for 25 minutes.

It is not about having time for family,
It is about…
Making Time for **FAMILY**

Taco Quiche

1 lb. ground beef
1 env. taco seasoning mix
4 eggs
3/4 C. milk
1 1/2 C. Quick and Easy Biscuit Mix
Desired taco toppings

Brown meat in a skillet; drain. Stir in taco seasoning mix. Spoon mixture into greased 9x13 baking dish. Whisk eggs and milk. Add biscuit mix and stir until well combined. Pour over meat. Bake uncovered at 400 for 20-25 minutes or until golden brown. Cool 5-10 minutes. Serve with your favorite taco toppings, such as shredded cheese, sour cream, lettuce, tomatoes, peppers, onions, black olives, and salsa.

Mexican Dumplings

1 lb. ground beef, browned
2 C. salsa
1 15-oz. can kidney beans, undrained
1 15-oz. can whole-kernel corn, undrained
1 8-oz. can tomato sauce
2 tsp. chili powder, divided
1 1/2 C. biscuit mix
1/2 C. milk
1/2 C. shredded colby-jack cheese

In a large saucepan, combine beef, salsa, beans, corn, tomato sauce, and 1 tsp.chili powder. Bring to a boil. Stir remaining chili powder, biscuit mix, and milk. Drop dough into 6 mounds onto boiling beef mixture. Reduce temperature to low. Cover; cook 20 minutes or until dumplings are light and fluffy. Sprinkle with cheese. Cook 2 minutes more or until cheese is melted.

Pancakes

2 C. biscuit mix
2 C. water
2 eggs, well beaten

Fluff biscuit mix with a whisk or fork. Whisk in eggs and water until just moistened. Drop onto hot, lightly greased griddle. Cook until tiny bubbles appear over top of pancake. Flip and cook opposite side.

Deluxe Waffles

2 C. biscuit mix
2 C. water
1 tsp. vanilla extract
2 eggs, separated

Fluff biscuit mix with a whisk or fork. Stir in water, vanilla, and egg yolks until just blended. Beat egg whites to soft-peak stage. Fold into batter. Pour batter into greased, heated waffle iron. Cook until golden brown.

Tuna Gravy and Waffles

Make a white sauce from page 67. Stir in 1-2 cans tuna (drained) and 1 C. fresh or frozen green peas. Heat through. Serve over waffles.

German Pancakes

6 T. butter
6 eggs, beaten
1 C. milk
1 C. all-purpose flour
1/2 tsp. salt

Heat oven to 425 degrees. Melt butter in 9x13 baking dish. Beat remaining ingredients. Pour over melted butter. Bake 15-20 minutes or until edges are browned.

French Crepes

1 1/2 C. all-purpose flour
2 C. milk
2 large eggs
1 tsp. salt
1 T. sugar
Butter for cooking

In a large bowl, whisk all ingredients except butter until there are no lumps. Let rest 30 minutes. Heat crepe pan or skillet over medium-high heat. Melt enough butter to lightly coat pan. Pour 1/3 C. batter into center of pan. Lift and swirl to coat pan with batter. Cook until edges start to brown; carefully turn crepe and cook until slightly crispy around edges and browned at the center. Transfer to plate. Continue cooking crepes, adding a little more butter to the pan every 3-4 crepes.

Dinner Crepes or Waffles:
Make a dinner buffet with cooked hamburger or sausage, gravy, shredded cheese, and sautéed veggies (such as onions, peppers, zucchini, or mushrooms) and layer with crepes or waffles.

Creamy Ham Crepes

8-12 thin slices ham

8-12 French crepes

1 C. shredded cheese

2 C. Alfredo sauce

Place a slice of ham on each crepe and sprinkle with shredded cheese. Roll up and place in a greased 9x13 baking dish. Pour Alfredo sauce over crepes. Sprinkle with remaining cheese. Bake at 400 for 15-20 minutes or until cheese is melted and bubbly.

Chicken Spinach Crepes

1 onion, finely diced

2 T. butter

3 C. chopped, cooked chicken breast

1 bunch spinach

1 C. Alfredo sauce

1/2 C. sliced green onions (optional)

8-12 French crepes, warm

1 C. shredded Parmesan cheese

Sauté diced onion in butter until onions start to brown. Stir in chicken, spinach, Alfredo sauce, and green onions, Cook and stir until spinach is tender and sauce is hot and bubbly. Sprinkle with salt and pepper. Spread chicken filling down centers of warm crepes. Sprinkle with Parmesan cheese. Roll up and serve immediately.

1 C. water
1 stick butter
1/4 tsp. salt
1 C. all-purpose flour
4 large eggs

In a medium saucepan, bring water, butter, and salt to a boil. Add flour all at once, stirring quickly. Stir and cook until dough pulls away from sides of pan and starts to form a ball, about 1 minute. Remove from heat; cool 5 minutes. Beat in eggs until dough is smooth and glossy. Drop by heaping spoonfuls onto baking sheet to make 12-15 rolls. Bake at 450 for 10 minutes. Reduce temperature to 350 and bake 15-18 minutes more or until shells are crispy on the outside and set. Cool completely. Slice in half and spoon out soft insides. Fill with sandwich filling, such as chicken, tuna, or egg salad.

Tuna Salad Puffs

1 can tuna fish, drained
1/2 C. mayonnaise or salad dressing
3 dill pickles, finely diced
2 tomatoes, finely diced
2 C. chopped lettuce
Salt and pepper to taste

Combine all ingredients. Fill cooled and cut sandwich puffs with tuna filling.

Variations: Substitute 1 1/2 C. chopped cooked chicken or turkey for the tuna in this recipe. Substitute 6 hard-boiled eggs (peeled and chopped) for the tuna. Omit lettuce and tomatoes. Sprinkle with paprika.

Easy Tortillas

2 C. all-purpose flour
1/2 tsp. salt
3 T. butter
3/4 C. milk

Combine flour and salt; set aside. Heat butter and milk until just melted; combine with flour mixture. Sprinkle work surface with flour. Knead dough for a few minutes until smooth. Add flour if dough is sticky. Wrap with plastic wrap and let rest at room temperature for 30 minutes. Cut dough into 6 pieces; roll into balls. Roll out on lightly floured surface until very thin. Heat 1 T. oil in a pan over medium-high heat. Place one tortilla at a time in the pan. Cook tortilla 10 seconds, then flip over. Continue to flip every 10 seconds until the bubbles are golden.

*Note: Temperature should be hot enough to make tortillas bubble up quickly. You don't want to cook them too long, or they will be tough. Stack cooked tortillas; the moisture helps soften the surface, making them even more pliable.

Whole-Wheat Tortillas

2 C. whole-wheat flour
1 tsp. salt
2 T. butter or lard
6 oz. hot water

Place all ingredients in a mixer. Mix for 8–10 minutes. Let rest 1 hour. Divide into 8 balls. Roll out to desired thickness. Cook in a dry or lightly oiled skillet (cast iron works best) or on a griddle over medium-high heat. Cook as directed above.

Pocket Pita Bread

- 1 C. warm water
- 1 T. active dry yeast
- 2 1/2 to 3 C. all-purpose flour
- 2 tsp. salt
- 2 T. butter or lard
- Cooking oil

In a mixer or large bowl, mix water and yeast. Add 2 1/2 C. flour, salt, and butter or lard. Knead dough in mixer on medium speed or by hand 5-7 minutes or until dough is smooth and elastic. Add more flour if dough is sticky, but be careful; it's better to use too little flour than too much. Cover and let rise until double in size. Divide dough into 8 balls. Roll out on lightly floured surface to about 1/4 inch thickness. Heat 1 T. oil in a skillet over medium-high heat. Place one pita at a time in the pan. Cook 1 minute. Flip pita and cook 1-2 minutes or until golden. Repeat with remaining pitas. Cut pitas in half to make pockets.

Indian Fry Bread

- 2 C. all-purpose flour
- 1/4 C. cornmeal (optional)
- 1/4 C. powdered milk
- 4 tsp. baking powder
- 1/2 tsp. salt
- 2 T. oil
- 1 C. water

Whisk dry ingredients. Add oil and enough water to make a workable dough. Let dough rest 5-10 minutes. Divide into 2-inch balls. Stretch or roll balls until very thin. Fry in hot oil on both sides. Place on paper towels to drain excess oil. Use for Navajo Tacos.

Original Cornbread

1 C. flour
1 C. cornmeal
1 tsp. salt
1 T. baking powder
1/2 C. sugar
1 egg
1/4 C. oil
1 C. milk

Sift dry ingredients; set aside. Combine eggs, oil, and milk. Stir into dry ingredients until just blended. Pour into greased 9x13 baking dish. Bake at 400 for 20 minutes or until golden brown. For muffins, place paper cupcake liners in a cupcake pan. Pour batter to fill cups 2/3 full. Bake at 400 for 12-15 minutes. Serve with chili or bean dishes.

Sweet Cornbread

2 C. flour
1 C. cornmeal
1 tsp. salt
1 1/2 T. baking powder
1 C. sugar
3 eggs
1/2 C. oil or melted butter
2 C. milk

Sift dry ingredients; set aside. Combine eggs, oil, and milk. Stir into dry ingredients until just blended. Pour into greased 9x13 baking dish. Bake at 400 for 20 minutes or until golden brown. For muffins, place paper cupcake liners in a cupcake pan. Pour batter to fill cups 2/3 full. Bake at 400 for 12-15 minutes. Delicious with ham or cream soups.

Hush Puppies

Original Cornbread batter
1 onion, chopped
Oil for frying

Combine cornbread batter and chopped onion. Heat oil to about 350 degrees. Drop a small amount of batter into oil to test if the oil is hot enough. Drop a heaping tablespoon of batter at a time into hot oil. Turn to cook until all sides are browned. Place on paper towels to drain excess grease. Working with 5-8 hush puppies at a time, repeat this process until all of the batter is cooked. Serve with tartar sauce.

Corn Dog Bites

1 package hot dogs
Flour for dusting
Original Cornbread batter
Oil for frying
Ketchup
Mustard

Cut hot dogs into quarters. Stick a toothpick into each cut hot dog. Dip hot dog bites into flour to dust, then into carnbread batter, then immediately into hot oil. Turn until browned completely. Place on paper towels to drain excess grease. Working with 5-8 hotdog bites at a time, repeat this process until all bites are cooked. Serve with ketchup and mustard.

Fried Zucchini Sticks:
Follow above recipe but replace hot dogs with strips of zucchini the size of French fries. Dust in flour; dip in batter and cook as directed. Serve with ranch dressing or dip.

Veggie Cornbread Casserole

1 onion, diced
1/4 C. butter
1/4 C. water
3-4 C. chopped spinach or zucchini
6 eggs, well beaten
Salt and pepper to taste
1 C. shredded cheddar cheese
Original or Sweet Cornbread batter

Sauté diced onion in butter. Stir in water and spinach or zucchini. Steam-fry until spinach wilts or zucchini is crisp-tender. Spread into a greased 9x13 baking dish. Pour eggs over veggies. Sprinkle with salt and pepper and shredded cheese. Pour cornbread batter over top. Bake at 350 for 40-45 minutes or until top is set when lightly touched.

Tamale Pie

1 lb. ground beef
1 onion, chopped
15-oz. can diced tomatoes
15-oz. can black beans, drained and rinsed
1 14.5-oz. can whole-kernel corn, drained
1 T. chili powder
1 tsp. salt
1 tsp. garlic powder
1 1/2 C. shredded cheddar cheese
Tamale batter from opposite page

Brown ground beef with onion; drain grease. Combine all ingredients except cheese and tamale batter in a 9x13 baking dish. Sprinkle with cheese. Spread batter over top. Cover tightly with foil. Bake at 350 for 40 minutes. Let rest 10-15 minutes before serving.

Shredded Meat Tamales

3- to 4-lb. pork and/or beef roast
6 C. water
5 garlic cloves, minced
3 1/2 tsp. salt, divided
2 T. fresh-ground dried red chilis
1 28-oz. can enchilada sauce, divided
50 dried corn husks (about 8" long)
6 C. masa harina flour
1 1/2 tsp. baking powder
3/4 C. butter, lard, or shortening

Place roast, water, garlic, and 1 1/2 tsp. salt in slow-cooker. Cover and cook on high 3–4 hours or low 7–8 hours or until meat is very tender. Remove meat from broth and allow meat and broth to cool. Shred meat using 2 forks; discard fat and reserve for masa. Strain and reserve broth. Return meat to slow-cooker. Grind dried red chilis in a blender until it makes a powder. Stir in ground chilis and 2 C. enchilada sauce. Cover and simmer on low until masa is ready. Soak corn husks in warm water 20 minutes; drain well. Meanwhile, sift masa harina, baking powder, and remaining 2 tsp. salt. Cut in reserved fat and enough butter, lard, or shortening to make 3/4 C. Add remaining enchilada sauce and enough broth to make a thick, creamy paste.

Spread 2–3 T. masa down center of corn husk (each husk should be 8 inches long and 6 inches wide at the top; if husks are small, overlap 2 small husks to form 1.) Place 2 T. meat mixture in the middle of the masa. Fold in sides of husk and fold up the bottom. Tear thin strips (1/4 inch wide) from a husk. Use these as you would string to secure the tamales. Lean tamales in a steam basket, open side up. Add water to pot just below the steam basket. Bring water to a boil; reduce heat. Cover and steam 40 minutes, adding water when needed. To freeze, leave tamales in husks and place them in freezer bags. To reheat, thaw and wrap in a wet paper towel and reheat in the microwave for 2 minutes.

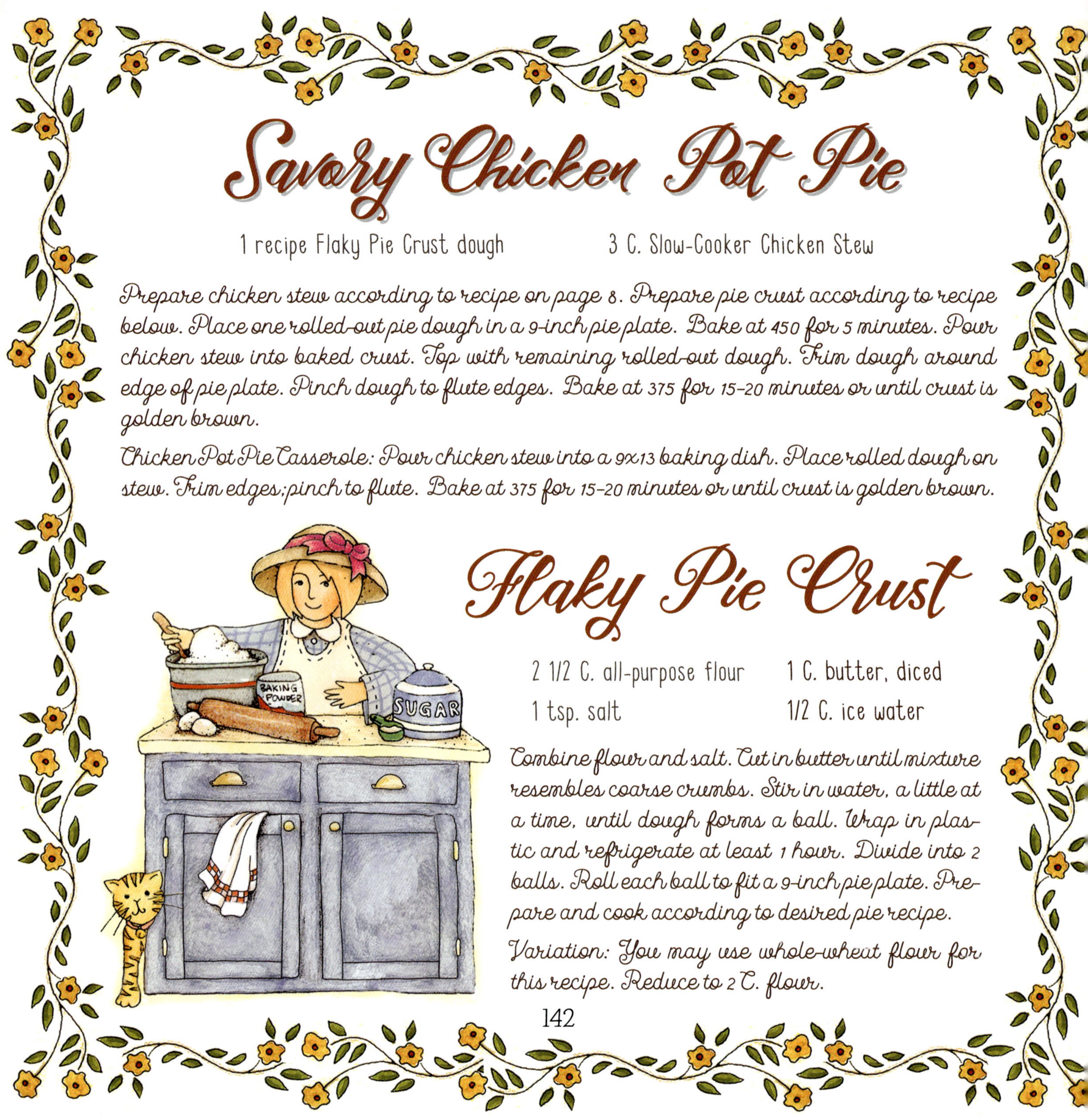

Savory Chicken Pot Pie

1 recipe Flaky Pie Crust dough
3 C. Slow-Cooker Chicken Stew

Prepare chicken stew according to recipe on page 8. Prepare pie crust according to recipe below. Place one rolled-out pie dough in a 9-inch pie plate. Bake at 450 for 5 minutes. Pour chicken stew into baked crust. Top with remaining rolled-out dough. Trim dough around edge of pie plate. Pinch dough to flute edges. Bake at 375 for 15-20 minutes or until crust is golden brown.

Chicken Pot Pie Casserole: Pour chicken stew into a 9x13 baking dish. Place rolled dough on stew. Trim edges; pinch to flute. Bake at 375 for 15-20 minutes or until crust is golden brown.

Flaky Pie Crust

2 1/2 C. all-purpose flour
1 tsp. salt
1 C. butter, diced
1/2 C. ice water

Combine flour and salt. Cut in butter until mixture resembles coarse crumbs. Stir in water, a little at a time, until dough forms a ball. Wrap in plastic and refrigerate at least 1 hour. Divide into 2 balls. Roll each ball to fit a 9-inch pie plate. Prepare and cook according to desired pie recipe.

Variation: You may use whole-wheat flour for this recipe. Reduce to 2 C. flour.

Meat Extender Ideas

Add 1 C. of cooked rice to 1 quart sloppy joe meat filling. Simmer 10-15 minutes or until rice has taken on the flavor of the sauce. Or add 1 C. water and 1/2 C. uncooked rice to 1 quart sloppy joe meat filling. Bring to a boil. Reduce temperature and simmer 25-30 minutes or until rice is tender.

Combine 1/4 C. cornmeal, quick oats, or bread crumbs to every pound ground beef when making hamburger pattties, meatballs, spaghetti sauce, or in your favorite casseroles.

Turn your favorite stews into mini pot pies. Press uncooked pie crust or flour tortillas into muffin cups. Fill with desired stew. Fold tortilla or pie crust over stew and pinch edges to seal. Bake at 350 for 15-20 minutes or until tops are browned.

In a family, Love is spelled...

T*I*M*E

Budget-Saving Tip

Breakfast has become a huge expense in the food budget over the past decade, but it doesn't need to be. Cold cereal costs between $3 and $5 per pound compared to things like homemade cereals, muffins, and pancakes, which cost an average of $.50 per pound.

Quick No-Bake Granola

- 1/4 C. butter
- 1/3 C. sugar
- 1/4 C. honey or brown sugar
- 1/3 C. milk
- 1/3 C. peanut butter
- 2-3 C. quick oats
- 1/3 C. raisins (optional)
- 1/3 C. coconut (optional)

Melt butter. Stir in sugar, honey, and milk. Bring to a boil and continue stirring for 2 minutes. Remove from heat and stir in peanut butter, oats (to desired texture), raisins if desired, and coconut if desired. Let cool 15-30 minutes before serving.

Variation: For crispy granola, spread cereal on ungreased baking sheet. Broil on top rack 2-3 minutes or until it begins to brown. Stir; repeat broiling process until raisins are plump and granola is crispy. Cool completely before serving.

Raisin Bran Cereal

- 1 C. bran
- 1 C. whole-wheat flour
- 1/4 C. sugar
- 1/2 tsp. baking soda
- 1/2 tsp. salt
- 2/3 C. water

Combine all ingredients. Pour into a greased sheet-cake pan. Spread evenly to sides of pan. Bake at 300 for 20 minutes. Turn temperature off but leave cereal in oven 10 additional minutes. Cool completely. Break into flakes.

Wheat-Nuts Cereal

3 1/2 C. whole-wheat flour
1 tsp. salt
1 tsp. baking soda
1 1/2 C. buttermilk
1/2 C. barley malt syrup

Combine flour, salt, and baking soda. Add buttermilk and barley malt syrup; mix just until evenly combined. Spread batter onto a greased sheet-cake pan; smooth out to the edges as evenly as possible. Bake at 350 until edges begin to brown and pull away from the pan, about 20 minutes. Loosen with a spatula and immediately turn out onto a cooling rack. Allow to cool 40–45 minutes. Break cake into chunks and pulse in food processor into desired-size pieces. Spread processed pieces evenly on 2 baking sheets Bake at 275, stirring every 15 minutes, until cereal is completely dry (about 45 minutes). Turn temperature to off, crack oven door, and allow to cool in oven. Store in an airtight container.

Cracked-Wheat Cereal

2 C. water
2/3 C. cracked wheat
1/2 tsp. salt
1/3 C. sugar or honey

Bring water to a boil. Stir in cracked wheat, salt, and sugar or honey. Reduce heat and simmer 5 minutes. Serve with milk.

If you don't have cracked wheat, place whole wheat in a blender and grind until you get a coarse, ground texture.

French Toast Casserole

12 slices bread, cubed
12 large eggs, well beaten
1 C. milk
1/2 C. sugar
3 T. cinnamon
1 tsp. vanilla

Place bread in buttered 9x13 baking dish. Whisk remaining ingredients until well beaten. Pour over bread. Cover and refrigerate overnight. Bake at 350 for 25-30 minutes or until golden brown. Drizzle with hot maple syrup just before serving.

Apple Cinnamon French Toast

Combine 2 C. chopped apples, 1/2 C. brown sugar, and 1 T. cinnamon. Follow above recipe for French toast. After refrigerating overnight, fold in apple mixture. Bake as directed. Drizzle with maple syrup or cream cheese icing.

Blueberry French Toast

Follow above recipe for French toast. After refrigerating overnight, fold 1 C. fresh blueberries into French toast mixture. Bake as directed. Drizzle with hot maple syrup and cream cheese icing.

Day-Old Bread Pudding

4 C. cubed day-old bread
1 C. sugar
6 large eggs, well beaten
2 C. milk
2 tsp. vanilla
1/2 C. brown sugar
2 T. cinnamon (optional)
1/2 stick butter
2 apples, chopped (optional)
1 C. raisins (optional)

Sauce Ingredients:
1 C. sugar
1 stick butter, melted
1 egg, beaten
2 tsp. rum extract

Place day-old bread cubes in a greased 9x13 baking dish. Combine sugar, eggs, milk, and vanilla. Pour over bread and let sit for 10 minutes. Meanwhile, mix brown sugar, cinnamon, and butter. Top with apples and raisins if desired. Sprinkle over bread mixture and bake at 350 for 35–45 minutes, or until set. Remove from oven.

For the sauce: Combine sugar, butter, and egg in a saucepan. Cook and stir over medium heat until sugar dissolves and sauce thickens. Add rum extract; cook and stir 1 minute more. Pour over bread pudding. Serve warm or cold.

These recipes are a great way to use old bread instead of letting it go to waste. The recipes work for both homemade and store-bought bread: be aware that homemade bread goes stale much more quickly than store-bought bread because there are no preservatives in it.

Recipes and Notes

Recipes and Notes

Index